THE BEST OF BOOK BONANZA

Lee Bennett Hopkins

HOLT, RINEHART AND WINSTON
New York   Chicago   San Francisco   Dallas
Montreal   Toronto   London   Sydney

To
Misha Arenstein—Teacher Supreme,
and
Madeline Romano Illyn, Associate Editor,
Teacher Magazine—
two special people who are more
than one hopes for in life.

Cover photo: HRW photo by Russell Dian
Part I: HRW photo by Vivian Fenster
Part II: Arthur Singer
Part III: Photo by Ken Wittenberg
Part IV: Photo by Florida News Bureau, Department of Commerce
Part V: Photo by National Education Association/Carl Purcell
Part VI: Photo courtesy Moore Public Schools, Moore, OK
Part VII: HRW photo by John King
Part VIII: Photo by Suzanne Szasz

Library of Congress Cataloging in Publication Data

Hopkins, Lee Bennett.
  The best of Book bonanza.

  Based on selections from the column, Book
bonanza, which appears monthly in Teacher magazine.
  Includes bibliographical references.
  1. Books and reading for children.
2. Children's literature—Book reviews.
I. Teacher. II. Title.
Z1037.A1H66   028.52   79-20668
ISBN 0-03-052681-7 (paper)
ISBN 0-03-056714-9 (cloth)

Preface

The Best of Book Bonanza is for everyone interested in bringing children and books together. The volume's emphasis is on the everyday use of books in elementary and junior high school classrooms and libraries to create exciting and practical reading/literature environments. This collection stems from a monthly feature column, "Book Bonanza: All About Books Old and New and How To Use Them," which has appeared in *Teacher* magazine since November 1974. Herein, I have selected the best of the past six years, reedited, substantially reorganized, enlarged, and updated each of the topics.

It is my firm belief that books for children can and must become an integral part of the total school curriculum, weaving in and out of every subject area. Each chapter deals with a specific topic; within each chapter, recommended books in print are discussed that appeal to children and young adults to meet both reading and interest levels. Titles include current works as well as staple items in the field. A host of ideas and activities built around the topics are suggested; all of these have been successfully tried-and-tested in classrooms and libraries around the country.

Wherever possible, books of poetry or single poems are cited to aid in the integration of this important genre of literature as a natural, unforced part of children's life and learning. Professional references are also interspersed to guide educators further into specific studies.

References at the end of each chapter give complete bibliographic information—author, title, publisher, and copyright data; books available in paperback editions are also noted. The Appendix, *Publishers' Complete Addresses,* is included to facilitate ordering and/or for being placed on mailing lists to receive catalogues, book announcements, and other promotional materials to keep abreast of books and the publishing industry.

A great deal of help was offered to make such a volume possible and I should like to thank the following people, to whom I am greatly indebted:

Claudia Cohl, Editorial Director of Elementary Magazines, Scholastic Magazines and Book Services, who paved the way for "Book Bonanza"; Joan Sullivan Baranski, Editor of *Teacher* magazine, who has continued to give me support; Richard C. Owen, Senior Acquisitions Editor, John Mahaney, Education Editor, and Robin Gross, Project Editor, at Holt, Rinehart and Winston, who saw it through; my many friends in the publishing world, particularly juvenile promotion personnel who untiringly keep me abreast; the multitude of educators who constantly provide me with insight and ideas; and children throughout the country who love and share books with me.

Special appreciation must be given to Charles John Egita for his invaluable time and assistance in preparing the manuscript, and Marilyn E. Marlow, my agent at Curtis Brown, Ltd., for her constant encouragement.

Contents

PART 1

Books and and Children

The world of books for children and the people in it

Over the past two-decades-plus, I have been involved with children and children's books, and it never ceases to amaze me what a wide and ever-changing world it is. During this period of time, I have used children's books with those for whom they are intended—teachers, librarians, parents, and of course, children. My work in the field of education and writing has brought me into contact with girls and boys of all backgrounds and ages —from preschoolers and children in kindergarten, through elementary, junior and senior high school grades, and even college-aged students.

Quite early in the process, I became aware of an odd phenomenon about the industry of publishing books for children: Adults write and illustrate them, adults edit, design, and publish them, adults review and buy them; the last on the long receiving line are the children who finally get the product intended *for* them.

There are eight groups of people within the world of children's books—authors and illustrators, publishers and editors, reviewers, booksellers, librarians, teachers, parents, and children. Although each group is quite diverse, they all strive toward one purpose—to get children interested and involved in reading and in the love of books.

AUTHORS AND ILLUSTRATORS

Quite simply, authors are people who write books. The writing can assume many forms—picture books, novels, volumes of poetry, or one of the host of topics delineated as nonfiction, such as biography and informational books. Some authors work their entire lifetime within the framework of one form and/or genre; others crisscross the lines, producing various types of work.

An author's first goal is to complete a manuscript that will be published—to share the fruits of one's love and labor (in that order) with girls and boys.

I have had the rare privilege of interviewing close to 200 authors and illustrators of books for children. Each one is different and unique, not only in their professional craft but in their lifestyles as well. They live throughout the United States and world—some in huge houses, teeny houses, one-room studios, five-room duplexes; others live in cellar apartments where one has to walk down to enter, walk-ups where one has to climb up and up and up to get into, city brownstones, houses near the shore, ranches in Maine and Colorado; still others live in handmade houses, reconverted libraries and churches, and even in observation towers. They are involved in all aspects of life, from politics to theatre, advertising to camping. The one thing they have in common is that they draw upon their experiences and talents to reach their goal of producing books for children.

For some book-people writing and/or illustrating comes easily; others struggle through each and every creation. Walter Farley, the popular author of the *Black Stallion* series, compares the creation of his books to having a baby: "Conception. Initial thrill at its development. Drudgery as the months wear on. And postbirth blues." The incomparable Dr. Seuss has told me that to produce a 60-page book like *The Cat in the Hat,* which took well over one year to complete, he may easily write 1000 pages before he is satisfied. "I write, rewrite, reject, reject, and polish incessantly," he states. "Every time I start a new book, that cat squints at me and says, 'Seuss, I bet you can't top me!'"

Commenting on her work habits, the ever-popular Beverly Cleary told me, "I sit at my desk twirling around on a swivel chair, staring out the window and hoping some strange new bird will light on the plum tree so I will have an excuse to look it up in *Field Guide to Western Birds.* Some stories come out right the first time; others I rewrite several times." The poet David McCord stated, "Sometimes poems come to me full-blown—nonsense verse in particular. More often I work at them, rewriting for choice of words and for sound and smoothness."

Caldecott Award winner Peter Spier, whose meticulously designed drawings consist of hundreds of minute details executed in full color, first creates accurate pencil drawings, then goes on to do ink sketches and finally watercolors. A book easily takes him four months or more to create, working steadily about 16 hours a day. "Do you know what happened to me after I finished my second Mother Goose Book?" he once asked me. "I had to go out and buy a pair of glasses!"

The late Don Freeman had his own idiosyncracy. When a book deadline drew near, he would check into a hotel so as not to be distracted. He had completed books in hotels in San Francisco, New York City, Los Angeles, and a host of other places. His *Dandelion,* a humorous tale about a lion who decides to live up to his name, was done in a gloomy hotel room in Washington, D.C.

Book creators vary widely in their opinions regarding children and books. Some enjoy trying out ideas with children, some create works based on their own children's growing-up years, others never come into contact with them at all, writing from within and for themselves.

Sharing lifestyles and viewpoints about authors and their work is an enlightening experience for children and adults alike.[1]

All in all, authors and illustrators are people—people who have created more memorable characters, situations, and magnificent artwork than can be found in any other media anywhere.

PUBLISHERS AND EDITORS

Publishing houses are in the business of manufacturing and selling books. At the head of each children's book department there is an editor whose role is manifold. Not only do they see

[1]See Chapter 2, "Staying On Top of Children's Books," for resources to acquaint children with authors lives and works.

books from concept to the finished product, they often serve as mentor, psychologist, and occasionally even parental figures to many of their authors and illustrators. Editors must deal with individuals who are as different as their books. Each title must be treated differently from the last, each getting the attention it needs to make it complete.

Jean Karl, Vice-President and Director of Atheneum's Children's Book Department, comments in her book, *From Childhood to Childhood: Children's Books and Their Creators* (John Day, 1970, page 92), "... a good editor of children's books cherishes every book.... Each is looked upon as an entity in itself.... In a good list, the books are individual, and they look individual. If for some reason an editor knows she cannot give a book the treatment it needs, she will be wise not (to) take it."

A book for children goes through many, many hands and stages, taking as long as one to three years before it is launched on the mass marketplace. The editor's role is to carefully oversee everything involved in the production, right up to the second it is born—and even afterwards. He or she is certainly one of the most important people throughout the total creative process of bookmaking.

Ann Durrell, Vice-President and Director of E. P. Dutton's Children's Book Department, summed up her role as an editor in a talk given at the Fifteenth Annual Symposium on children's literature sponsored by the University of California Berkeley's School of Library and Information Studies and Extension Division, in July 1977:

> The editor, who wields power over the whole process of physical production of a book from start to finish, must be the chief of those with whom the author is trying to communicate, perhaps one of the stimuli, indeed, to start the creative process moving. And once that work is completed, the editor is the first and most crucial judge of it, the one who decides whether or not it will be made into a book.
>
> Having made that important decision, the editor must then help the author make the book as good as possible. And this requires empathy. As an editor, I have to be able to see what the author sees. I have to get into that mind somehow....
>
> I am the one who brings together all of the parts to make the whole. I also have to fit the pieces of the less exciting, less creative elements that can make or break a book. Like production, promotion, sales and office staff—all of those, every day, I have to keep, somehow, moving as a functioning team. My reward is the books

—not one book, but many. Not a single perfect book—that may never exist—but many different books to suit many different children.[2]

REVIEWERS

Reviewers express their personal opinions of books for children. Some are well qualified, immersed in their field, wise and perceptive; others are not! There are endless discussions about reviewing and criticism among adults, but I believe that children can and must be brought into this process of evaluating the printed word. Without the reader in mind, many reviewers fall flat, expressing elitist positions that influence but cannot enhance the reading of books by children.[3]

Mae Durham Roger, a senior librarian at the University of California and coordinator of the annual symposium on children's literature mentioned above, has stated:

We can't go home again, and we cannot walk in the shoes of children. The reviewer often sees the book from an adult point of view and assumes that the child will respond in the same way. . . .

. . .[A] review should be an examination of a book, looking at it for what it is and not for what it is not. The review should point out how and why a book succeeds or fails. The reviewer must accomplish this without telling the author how to write or the artist how to illustrate.

Reviewers cannot and will not always agree. . . .[4]

And Betsy Hearne, editor of children's books for *Booklist* in a talk at Booklist's Open Forum during the 1978 American Library Association Conference, astutely commented on the vast differences between reviewing and criticism of children's books:

One of the things that will help the cause of literary criticism . . . is to give more honor to popular reading as a totally different kind of achievement. Our library awards now are neither truly literary nor truly popular. Instead of having opposing camps of practical

---

[2]"The Creative Spirit and Children's Literature: A Symposium," *Wilson Library Bulletin,* (October 1978), pp. 146–151.

[3]See Chapter 2, "Staying On Top of Children's Books," for thoughts about reviewing and a listing of some of the major review media.

[4]"The Creative Spirit and Children's Literature: A Symposium," p. 170.

and theoretical who sniff at each other, there should be enough honor and encouragement to further both, for they are not in conflict. *Arilla Sundown* by Virginia Hamilton is never going to hit the children's best-seller list, and *How to Eat Fried Worms* by Thomas Rockwell is never going to win a literary award, but they both make vital contributions to children's literature. It's not a question of either/or, of setting one's merits against the other; it's a matter of valuing the merits—the necessity—of both.[5]

BOOKSELLERS

Most major bookstores carry a selection of children's books. Those on display include only a handful of the approximately 2000 books for children published each year. There is usually a line of popular paperback volumes, classics, and sure-fire titles that sell continuously year after year, such as books by Dr. Seuss and E. B. White. The bulk of sales of children's books go to school and public libraries. If publishers had to depend on sales from bookstores, which only account for about 8 percent of books sold, they would have to close their doors.

The ideal marriage to bridge the gap between educators, publishers, and booksellers would take place if all became more involved with one another. Where and when this does take place, exciting results occur. In one Westchester school, for example, a fifth-grade teacher takes his class to visit a local bookstore several times during the course of the school year. Both he and the children have become acquainted with the buyer, occasionally making well-received suggestions about personal favorites. The bookstore has witnessed a thriving spurt of business actually selling books to young readers rather than only to parents, grandparents, other relatives, and teachers. Such interaction gives books and reading further importance.

Other examples of this abound. Annually, under the guidance of Anneliese Gastrich, school librarian, the Westorchard Elementary School in Chappaqua, New York, stages a week-long book fair where as many authors and illustrators as possible (sometimes as many as 30), visit the school to meet with youngsters. During this well-planned event, students have the

[5]Betsy Hearne, "Reviewing and Criticism: A World of Difference," *Booklist* (September 1, 1978), p. 47.

opportunity to meet authors and illustrators to discuss the process of writing and book creation.

Children themselves engage in the planning. While every class in the school has the opportunity to meet three or four authors, a particular one is assigned to each class. The class then concentrates on reading as many books as possible by that author prior to his or her visit. Each class makes a poster to welcome "its" author. Members of a fifth-grade class become the official hosts, and pairs of students are assigned to find out about the author's life and works, to read as many of the books as they can, to visit in advance the classes the author will visit to acquaint the other children with the books, and finally, to be the author's guide for the day's event. To further the excitement, Ms. Gastrich involves Joan Ripley, owner of the local bookstore, The Second Story, who orders titles by the various authors so that children and their parents can buy them and have them autographed when the big day rolls around.

Commenting on the success of this project, Ms. Ripley states:

> The fair gives us a large number of sales we wouldn't ordinarily have. It provides free advertising. It has a continuing effect on our children's book sales. Children are coming into the store to purchase other books they saw at the fair and wanted. Many of them now seem to be spending their allowances on particular titles we had on display.
>
> It has extended our store outside its physical limits and we have succeeded in taking books into the community rather than waiting for the community to come to us. Mostly, it has given us a lot of satisfaction to know that we were part of an exciting educational experiment and provided a real service to our community.

LIBRARIANS

In the past few years, both school and public libraries have suffered tremendous budget cuts. This, coupled with inflation, has caused reduction of staffs, shortened hours of operation, and the closing of branches throughout the country, affecting both adults' and children's use of the library. Despite these problems, Mary Jane Anderson, Executive Secretary of the American Library Association's Children's Service Division, has commented that today's children are using libraries more than ever before.

The library is one of the most important institutions in any community, and it is the librarian who can make and keep reading an ongoing life activity. The ideal relationship between public and school librarians is one in which both share their varied resources and different types of expertise. The same holds true of librarian–teacher relationships.

The school library is an integral part of the entire school plant. The ideal school librarian shares in continuous classroom educational programs as well as in the academic and personal growth of all students.

Teachers can help in cementing these bonds. One important thing all teachers must do *on the very first day of school* when meeting new classes is to find out if children have a library card. Often, this is taken for granted. In a second-grade class in New York City, for example, one teacher found that only 12 out of 26 children owned this important document; in a small town in Missouri, a fourth-grade teacher found only 10 out of 25 students had a card.

Reasons for this are varied: Some children *never* had one; others lost theirs somewhere during their growing-up years and never bothered to get another one; still others are new arrivals into a community and they need to learn about the library and its services in their new environment. The importance of the few minutes that it takes to find out "who has" and "who has not"—even if there is only one who hasn't—need not be discussed. All of us well know that any child in any classroom without a library card is certainly missing out on a multitude of irreplaceable life experiences and treasures.

Once teacher–librarian connections are strong, the community can easily be drawn together. An exciting program to unite all community resources is the establishment of a Children's Reading Round Table where public and school librarians, professors of children's literature, authors, illustrators, booksellers, and parents come together to share a common interest in books for children.

One of the oldest Round Tables is the Chicago-based Children's Reading Round Table, organized in 1931, "to support activities which foster and enlarge children's interest in reading and to promote good fellowship among persons actively interested in the field of books for children." This is one of the few Round Tables that encourages membership from all over the country. Regular dues are $6.00 for those living within the Chicago area; dues for associates, limited to persons who are retired or living beyond the Chicago meeting area, are $3.50. By joining this most worthwhile association, you receive "Chicago Bulletin," published monthly September through May, an annual yearbook citing the history of the organization, a complete listing of members and their addresses, and the organizational bylaws which can aid in establishing a similar Round Table in your area. For information, write to Children's Reading Round Table, 1321 E. 56th Street, Chicago, Illinois 60606.

For those interested in keeping abreast of the library world —both public and school—the organization to belong to is the American Library Association. For membership information, write to the association at 50 East Huron Street, Chicago, Illinois 60611.

TEACHERS

The classroom teacher is the most influential individual when it comes to developing both reading habits and the true love for reading in children. Since *The Best of Book Bonanza* is teacher-oriented, I need not explain the importance of using books with children and truly getting them involved. I would rather cite several cornerstones to good teaching.

One of the most important points is that *every teacher, everywhere,* should read to his or her class *everyday.* This is usually an automatic experience in primary grades, but middle-grade teachers often tell me they do not have the time to spare for such a routine. The time *must* be found—even if it is only 10 minutes per day. The contribution that reading aloud makes to children's literacy and language skills, as well as the appreciation for books and the reading process per se, cannot be overemphasized. Study after study has proven that when children have had a steady diet of hearing books read aloud to them, their enthusiasm, understanding, and love for books has greatly increased.

Today, far too much emphasis is placed on formal accountability. Despite the fact that most teachers have always been accountable and have always attempted to do the most for every child, valuable classroom teaching time is being spent, and wasted, on "clerical duties." Formal tests and their results are fine in measuring conceptual growth, in telling teachers what has been missed by students. But how does one measure enthusiasm and enjoyment? I have never found a test for these abstracts; yet, that is what reading and the love of reading are all about. Evaluation ought to be concerned with both, if it is serious. Accountability and testing can sometimes become distorted!

Over the years, I have seen endless guides written by well-meaning educators that ask question after question about particular stories and/or poems to "test" children's comprehension. One guide, for example, listed 91 questions "for comprehension" about *Charlotte's Web*! This averages out to approximately one question per every two pages of print! The fact that boys and girls can be taught to answer question after question does not measure the book's validity, nor does it evaluate the book's impact. I have read *Charlotte's Web* aloud to children many times over, and I have seen some children openly cry, while other "hardcores" struggle to keep tears from flowing. Each time this occurs, this magic, I know that E. B. White's beautiful language and message has touched them like they have never been touched before. I do not need to ask a host of banal questions—and never shall. All this does is destroy the love of reading—any type of reading.

In a speech given at the 1978 National Council of Teachers of English Language Arts Conference in Phoenix, Arizona, Charlotte S. Huck remarked, "My goal for schools would be to develop not only children who know how to read but children who do read, who find pleasure in books and are well on their way to becoming lifetime readers." Huck's statement links "knowing and loving" what is inside a book quite well. This is the ultimate reading objective!

PARENTS

The movement to get parents involved in children's reading is more on the move today than ever before. While teachers have long recognized the importance of parental support in day-to-day classroom matters, much of today's new emphasis is keyed toward involving mothers and fathers in new ways.

In late 1977, the Children's Book Council invited proposals from libraries, educators, booksellers, and others as to how children's books might be brought to the attention of parent groups. The invitation came from the Council's Parent Activities Committee, which offered grants of $500 to a limited number of institutions or individuals that might suggest interesting and innovative ways to inform parents about children's books.

The committee received close to 400 proposals. From these, seven were selected to receive grants. Three of the programs initiated include:

Los Angeles, California, Public Library: Children's Room

For a series of 10 half-hour sessions, related to integrating children's books into family life, offered in the Children's Room at noontime.

Persons attending would be adults employed in the vicinity of the Central Library, located in a district of Los Angeles with a heavy concentration of businesses and high-rise office buildings. Those attending will hear specialists talking about books to help with common, childhood problems, reading readiness, and books for reluctant readers. Each session will be independent of others in the series, and booklists on the subject of the day will be distributed.

Area office buildings will receive flyers about the sessions. Plans will also be made to have the *Los Angeles Times* announce the subject of each session, and to have a bookseller agree to sell, at the library, copies of each book mentioned at the programs. It is also expected that one or more of the businesses close to the Central Library will cosponsor the sessions to defray some of the costs not covered by the Children's Book Council grant.

Children's Reading Round Table (CRRT), Boise, Idaho

For a program by the Boise Public Library, The Bookshop (Boise) and the Boise Chapter of CRRT. The program is directed to fathers in the community.

Thirty to 35 fathers will meet monthly at the library for a discussion, moderated by a CRRT member, of at least five titles that will have been read by fathers to their children in Idaho's "Read to Your Child 15 Minutes a Day" program. Between 60 and 70 titles, from preschool through junior high levels, will be selected by the Boise Public Library and the Bookshop staffs for the program. All books discussed during the series will be available from the library and The Bookshop.

Division of Educational Planning and Support, Center for Library, Media and Telecommunications, Board of Education of New York City, Brooklyn, New York

For a program designated, "Parents as Partners" (PAP) and focusing on the theme, "Children, Parents, and Reading."

Six workshops for 25 parents, one from each school in district 13 in Brooklyn, New York, a densely populated urban community. The workshops will feature these topics:

- introducing books to children during the early years
- selecting appropiate books to read to and with children
- motivating children to read
- building an inexpensive collection of children's books for the home
- sharing library use experiences
- parents as reading guides

At the conclusion of the workshops, each participating parent will be encouraged to organize a similar or adapted PAP program for other parents in the school he or she represents.

Acquainting parents with the world of children's books is indeed a multifaceted task. A few first steps, however, can get them to think about and know books and their importance to child development.

Either on parent nights at school or via Parent–Teacher–Association newsletters, urge all parents to:

1. Get to know the school and public librarian and ask for specific help in choosing books for children.
2. Meet with the child's teacher and ask for titles and authors that meet specific age or interest levels.
3. Encourage parents, both mothers and fathers, to join their children in reading carefully selected books.
4. Visit a good bookstore with children to buy books for a home library.

Two excellent aids which all parents should be acquainted with and will welcome knowing about are Nancy Larrick's *A Parent's Guide to Children's Reading* (Bantam paperback) and *Parents' Choice: Review of Children's Media.* Larrick's book, now in its fourth edition, discusses such important topics as how parents can help children and reading on a day-in, day-out basis; how to use a library; how to build a home library; and advice on buying books for children.

Parents' Choice, a welcome and long-overdue newcomer, is a newspaper published bimonthly. It features: 1) a wide range of articles written by educators, authors of children's books, and parents; 2) several excellent features discussing and reviewing children's books, recordings, movies, television shows, and toys; and 3) a column, "Good and Cheap," listing inexpensive paperback volumes for children from preschool through age 12.

For subscription information, write to Parents' Choice, Box 185, Waban, Massachusetts 02168. Don't hesitate to steer all parents toward these resources.

CHILDREN

Today, despite all the talk about television taking the place of reading in children's lives, most youngsters still find that everyday life requires them to read both in and out of school. Some places lack the enthusiasm that can and should be part of any reading program. Forward-looking educators motivate rather than simply require children to read; they do this by offering readers a broad spectrum of books dealing with subjects that are meaningful to students as individuals. It matters little whether they are past-classics or contemporary themes. Active readers can be taught to select books they find appealing, from all periods of time—from all genre of literature. The following approaches are a small sampling of techniques teachers use to lead youngsters into books and literary appreciation.

An exciting project in literature is to have students establish an award based on *their* choices of favorite books. Currently, there are approximately 16 such awards sponsored by school and library associations from New England to Hawaii.[6]

A national list, "Classroom Choices: Books Chosen by Children," is published annually and compiled under the direction of the International Reading Association–Children's Book

---

[6]For a complete listing, see Charlotte S. Huck, *Children's Literature in the Elementary School,* 3d ed. (New York: Holt, Rinehart and Winston, 1979), pp. 765–766.

Council Joint Committee to aid teachers, librarians, and parents in identifying those books that children themselves love. Of the more than 2000 children's trade books published, approximately 500, chosen for their inherent excellence and diversity of types and subjects, are preselected by a group of educators. Publisher members of the Children's Book Council then send these books to each of five teams who use the books in classrooms across the nation. Each team—consisting of a children's literature specialist at a university, plus one or more classroom teachers—tests a minimum of 2000 children in the field; thus, at least 10,000 children from throughout the country are engaged in selecting these books. Records of the children's reactions are kept, with preliminary screening of the list done in January and March. In late April, the teams meet to record the final selections for the new "Classroom Choices." And it is the children's choices that count; it is their vote that elects a book to the bibliography or keeps it off. To obtain a reprint of the current "Children's Choices," send a self-addressed stamped envelope to the Children's Book Council, Attention: "Children's Choices," affixing appropiate postage for two ounces.

Acquainting colleagues, parents, and children with such projects might well spark a similar program in your own classroom, school, community, city or state if it doesn't already exist. Children should have their say about books written for them; this is one way to hear young voices.

Also, encourage children to subscribe to *Cricket: The Magazine for Children,* published monthly by The Open Court Publishing Company, 1058 Eighth Street, LaSalle, Illinois, or to seek it out in the school or public library. This excellent periodical features writing and illustrations from the best in the world of children's books. Each issue contains excerpts from books and regular features such as "Meet Your Author," reviews of current titles, and "The Cricket League," inviting girls and boys to enter story, poetry, and drawing contests based on specific themes. It is by far the best of the children's magazines available on the marketplace today.

In sum, my experiences in teaching, writing, speaking about books, and meeting children throughout America confirm my strong belief that boys and girls are indeed capable of finding much that is great in books. It is hoped that this volume will help to bring children and books together—the most basic of basics for today—and always!

Staying on top of children's books

Each year, an estimated 2000 books for children roll off the presses. Add the approximately 40,000 previously published inprint backlist titles to that, and you have a veritable mountain of materials to sort through and seek out. This certainly is not an easy task for any educator—teacher or librarian.

To help bring children and books together effectively, refer often to the following books and periodicals, especially when you are planning lessons, embarking on new subject territory, or trying to meet your student's special interests with books. Share your discoveries with colleagues, librarians, and parents, and ask for their recommendations. The time you invest will help you get a firmer hold on the constantly changing world of children's literature.

THE BIG TWOSOME

Two volumes—the "bibles" of the field—that you will find yourself using and referring to again and again are *Children's Literature in the Elementary School* by Charlotte S. Huck, and *Children and Books* by Zena Sutherland and May Hill Arbuthnot. Both cover the entire scope of children's literature from the earliest books ever published to contemporary volumes. Constantly revised and updated to acquaint readers with the newest of the new, the third updated edition of Huck's volume was

17

published in 1979, the fifth edition of Sutherland and Arbuthnot's in 1977.

Whether you are looking for information on poetry, picture
books, fiction, or nonfiction, or suggestions for activities to get
children involved in literature, you will find what you want in
these texts, no matter what grade you teach. Each also contains
thick appendices of book awards, lists, selection aids, pronunciation guides, publisher's addresses, and subject, author, illustrator, and title indices.

"RIGHT NOW" INFORMATION

Due to the nature of the publishing industry, no book can
supply "right now" information. But there are several avenues
to explore if you want to keep up with what is happening in the
field.

One publication to keep close at hand is *The Calendar,* published by The Children's Book Council, 67 Irving Place, New
York, New York 10003. Appearing three times every two years,
it features articles about and interviews with people in the
publishing world. Regular and particularly useful features include "Up to Date with Books," which cites upcoming holidays
and special events listing related books which have appeared
within the past three years, and "Materials Available," which
provides information about free and inexpensive items that
you or your students can send away for, such as bookmarks by
the packet, posters, jacket illustrations, and author/illustrator
biographical sheets. A one-time fee of $5.00 puts you on the
mailing list forever!

Current information on news, reviews, and trends is also
available in a variety of periodicals. Each of the following
book-related publications has its own distinctive personality
and appeal. Therefore, you may want to look through copies in
your school or public library prior to ordering to determine
whether they meet your specific needs:

  • A subscription to *School Library Journal,* published
monthly, September through May, by R. R. Bowker Company,
P.O. Box 67, Whitinsville, Maine 01588, is $13.00 per year.
  • *The Horn Book,* 31 St. James Avenue, Boston, Massachu-
setts 02116, is published six times a year; $12.00.
  • For the most up-to-date reviews, steer toward *Booklist,* pub-

lished twice monthly, September through May and once in August; subscription rate is $28.00 per year through the American Library Association, 50 East Huron Street, Chicago, Illinois 60611.

• *The Bulletin of the Center of Children's Books* appears monthly except August for $10.00 per year from The University of Chicago Press, 5801 Ellis Avenue, Chicago, Illinois 60637.

One caution to keep in mind about reviews of any kind is that they are one person's opinion. You can gather many more by drawing your students into a book evaluation session after they have read a recently reviewed book and listening to their viewpoints. Then, read aloud one or several of the adult reviewers opinion. Do they agree or disagree? Encourage the children to serve as Junior Reviewers and promote writing skills at the same time by posting their "best-seller" recommendations on the bulletin board. This will be the final test of what makes a good book "good."

Many years ago, the late May Hill Arbuthnot shared an important point, stating: "Two facts we need to keep constantly before us: A book is a good book for children only when they enjoy it; a book is a poor book for children, even when adults rate it as a classic, if children are unable to read it or are bored by its content." Certainly this holds true today.

MEETING AUTHORS

When children get to know something about the lifestyles, work habits, and insights of authors and illustrators, they often enjoy their works more and seek out other titles by the same individuals. To fill in this background information for your students, try *More Books By More People* by Lee Bennett Hopkins. Sixty-five personal interviews are featured with contemporary authors and illustrators, including many of the Newbery award winners, plus poets, anthologists, and creators of nonfiction books. A black-and-white photograph of each of the personalities is included. Twenty-three interviews make up *The Pied Pipers,* another source, by Justin Wintle and Emma Fisher. The question-and-answer format focuses on such personalities as Laurent de Brunhoff, John Gardner, and Judy Blume.

Due to the number of books in the series (fifteen volumes to date at $25.00 each), *Something About the Author,* edited by Anne Commire, may not be readily available to you and your students. However, the entries for each author or illustrator are so comprehensive, including book illustrations and quotes, hobbies, and personal comments, that the collection is worth seeking out in a public library.

Fascinating portraits of authors who have written Newbery Medal or Newbery Honor Books are included in the unique, "Meet the Newbery Author" multimedia series produced by Miller–Brody. Addressed to child audiences, these full-color delights provide insight into the lives of the individuals, as well as serve as an introduction to other books they have created. For a complete listing of titles, write to the company for their complete catalogue.

A new series, "Self-Portraits," was launched in 1978, by Addison-Wesley. The first two volumes to appear were *Self-Portrait: Margot Zemach,* and *Self-Portrait: Erik Blevgad.* The easy-to-read text, excellent design of the volumes, and full-color illustrations answer such questions as how these talents work and where, where ideas and images come from, and how and where one begins getting into the business of becoming an artist of picture books. This is a series to know about, share with students of all ages, and look forward to for new "Self-Portraits" that will come our way.

BOOKS AND MEDIA

Reading Guidance in a Media Age by Nancy Polette and Marjorie Hamlin gives practical reasons and how-tos for establishing effective reading/media programs. A multitude of ideas are offered, including suggestions for developing independent study programs and learning packages, the use of drama and puppetry to stimulate reading, and the development of student audiovisual productions based on books. The last chapter, "Students, Teachers, Librarians and Authors Get Together," cites ways to do just that, including the planning, execution, and follow-up literature conferences.

A Multimedia Approach to Children's Literature, compiled and edited by Ellin Greene and Madalynne Schoenfeld, features a selected listing of nonprint media based on children's books through 1977. A directory of distributors and indices of authors, titles, and subjects are appended.

INTO THE HOME

To enlist parents' support for home reading or to answer the question, "What can we do to help our child?" you can suggest a book that is effectively designed for this purpose—*A Parent's Guide to Children's Reading* by Nancy Larrick. Now in its fourth edition, this classic not only lists recommended fiction, nonfiction, magazines, and audiovisual materials for all ages, but also explains how to foster a happy reading environment in the home, build a library, and evaluate children's books.

The best part of staying on top of the mountain of children's books is the view. With professional materials as your guide, the vista can be filled with scenes of happy reading.

REFERENCES[1]

Blevgad, Erik. *Self-Portrait: Erik Blevgad.* Addison-Wesley, 1979.

Commire, Anne, ed. *Something About the Author,* 15 vols. Gale Research Company.

Greene, Ellin, and Madalynne Schoenfeld. *A Multimedia Approach to Children's Literature,* 2d ed. American Library Association, 1977.

Hopkins, Lee Bennett. *More Books By More People.* Scholastic/Citation Press, 1974; also available in paperback.

Huck, Charlotte S. *Children's Literature in the Elementary School,* 3d ed. Holt, Rinehart and Winston, 1979.

Larrick, Nancy. *A Parent's Guide to Children's Reading.* Doubleday, 1975; Bantam paperback.

Polette, Nancy, and Marjorie Hamlin. *Reading Guidance in a Media Age.* Scarecrow Press, 1975

Sutherland, Zena, and May Hill Arbuthnot. *Children and Books.* Scott, Foresman, 1977.

Wintle, Justin, and Emma Fisher. *The Pied Pipers.* Paddington Press, 1974.

Zemach, Margot. *Self-Portrait: Margot Zemach.* Addison-Wesley, 1978.

[1]See Appendix for publishers' complete addresses.

PART II

Understanding Life

3

Age is one thing we all share

Sick, sad, tired, dirty, and *ugly:* These negative terms were frequently used by 180 children between the ages of 3 and 11 who participated in a year-long study. They were not surveyed on their feelings about junked cars, abandoned pets, or last year's toys. The children were describing their impression of the aged.

The University of Maryland's Center on Aging conducted the study with the school's Department of Early Childhood/Elementary Education. Edward F. Ansello, the center's associate director, notes that in 656 children's books that were also evaluated as part of the study, three words—*old, little,* and *ancient* —accounted for more than 80 percent of the adjectives used to describe the elderly.

It is difficult for many children to understand that aging is a natural process we all undergo. Certainly, the books they encounter that present stereotypical viewpoints do little to help. However, there are a number of activities and volumes you can consider to promote better understanding.

DEVELOPING NEW VIEWPOINTS

Since most children's contacts with the elderly are their grandparents, you might want to ask your students how much they really know about them as people. For example, are they employed or retired? What kind of work do or did they do? What are their hobbies, interests, and skills? What kinds of books and music do they like best? If the children are unable to answer questions such as these, suggest that they discuss them with their grandmother or grandfather or a neighbor or acquaintance who is a grandparent. This type of communication is just as important (if not more so) as the answers.

To further children's contacts with the aged, consider adapting one of the following programs for your classroom. In Merrick, New York, an annual "Grandparent's Day" is held during which both grandparents and members of the senior community spend a morning with the children in school. They share information about themselves or present specific skills they have acquired.

In a school district in Iowa, fourth, fifth and sixth graders become "Little Friends for Older Friends." Every week the children take a bus trip to senior housing areas, community centers, or churches to visit the elderly, followed up by phone calls, letters and an annual "Everyperson's Picnic!"

At holiday time in Appleton, Minnesota, third graders make gifts and present holiday programs for patients at a residence for the aged. Several classes in New York City hold "Grandparent Storytelling Days," during which grandparents come into classes to read or tell a favorite story on a weekly, biweekly, or monthly basis.

In an excellent article, "Teaching About Aging: You Owe It To Yourself,"[1] Sheila Sobell Moramarco offers many tried-and-tested activities to further youngsters' awareness of the aging process. A unique suggestion comes from Peggy Marketello, a California elementary school teacher who worked with fourth, fifth, and sixth graders. At the end of a unit on agism, her students gave a "Senility Award" to "the advertising company that most negatively portrayed aging in marketing their product." One year, the students gave the award to the Olay Company, Incorporated, in Wilton, Connecticut, distributors of the popular beauty lotion, Oil of Olay. Students wrote letters to the company protesting advertising techniques which they felt were derogatory to elder viewers. An activity such as this not only encompasses the five important components of the language arts—speaking, reading, writing, listening, and critical

[1]Sheila Sobell Moramarco, "Teaching About Aging: You Owe It To Yourself," *Learning* (March 1978), pp. 44–48.

thinking—but also ties in critical television viewing of advertising techniques used to sell and promote products.

An excellent resource for mature readers that will spark a great deal of discussion regarding views of the aged is *Tales of the Elders: A Memory Book of Men and Women Who Came to America as Immigrants, 1900–1930* by Carol Ann Bales. The handsomely designed volume, illustrated with black-and-white photographs, contains 12 short interviews with people who came to America during the "Great Migration" period. Their memories of how and why they traveled here, what they left behind, what they hoped for, what they did, and how they reconstructed their lives in a new country provide thoughtful reading.

VALUABLE RELATIONSHIPS

Children's books with positive views of the aged can be used to initiate, enhance, and follow up discussions and projects. In the following titles, girls and boys will not find the words *sick* or *sad* or even the proverbial *old!*

Two titles that beautifully depict loving grandparent/grandchild relationships are *A Little at a Time* by David A. Adler and *Grandpa and Me* by Patricia Lee Gauch. In *A Little at a Time,* a story told entirely in dialogue, a young boy asks his grandfather question after question during a city visit. His grandfather explains how things like tall trees, deep holes, and even small boys grow and change a little at a time. The gentle rhythmic words with illustrations by N. M. Bodecker make this an excellent read-aloud book. *Grandpa and Me* is a gently moving account of shared summertime experiences. A boy and his grandfather hike in the woods and on the beach, drink lemonade on the porch, and eat berries underneath the maple tree. When day is done, Grandpa says, "Let's trade stories. . . ."—and they do. Tinted wash illustrations by the master artist Symeon Shimin capture and enhance the delicate text.

The Shopping-Bag Lady, written and illustrated in two colors by cartoonist Robert Censoni, tells of an eccentric woman who cheerfully waddles from one end of the city to another poking into trash. Upon finding something she likes, she exclaims, "My, oh my, that must be something valuable!"—and pops it into her bag. Such habits make her the subject of children's taunts until they stumble upon the method to her "madness"—

the gala opening of her very own "The Valuable Antique Shop." This is a humorous volume to spark a serious discussion of how and why people behave as they do, whatever their age.

Differences of understanding between the generations are well handled in *Mandy's Grandmother* by Liesel Moak Skorpen, illustrated by Martha Alexander. Having never met her grandmother, Mandy has some definite rose-colored ideas—culled from a picture book—of what grandmothers should look like and how they should behave. Their first meeting produces an earthquake of shattered preconceptions. Not only does Grandma think Mandy is a boy, she also believes that oatmeal is for breakfast and that frogs don't make great pets. How the two begin to love and accept each other is warmly shown. A 16 mm., 30-minute color film based on the book is also available for rental or purchase from Phoenix Films, Inc., starring Maureen O'Sullivan and Amy Levitan.

Coping with Loss

The passing of a grandparent or another relative is often a child's first experience with death. Such a loss sometimes creates confusion, fear, and anxiety. Two books sensitively portray the subject and, in so doing, emphasize the importance of grandparents to the lives of those around them.

In *Nonna,* by Jennifer Bartoli, a family laughs as well as cries as they remember their grandmother who recently died. Her grandchildren in particular learn to treasure their sweet and sad memories of her, her gifts of love and joy for life. The story, told in the first person, is illustrated by Joan E. Drescher.

Charlotte Zolotow's *My Grandson Lew* is a perfect example of a picture book written with exquisite simplicity. It relates the story of a 6-year-old who wakes up in the middle of the night and tells his mother that he misses Grandpa, even though it has been four years since he died. To comfort each other, the two share memories of the man who brought so much love to their family. The tender full-color illustrations are by William Pène du Bois.

FOR THE PROFESSIONAL SHELF

To become more familiar and/or involved with organizations and services for the aged, send for free copies of the brochure, "Gray Panthers: Age and Youth in Action," and the national quarterly newspaper, *The Network,* by writing to the Gray Panthers, Inc. Another source is the paperback, *The New Old: Struggling for Decent Aging,* edited by Ronald and Beatrice Gross and Sylvia Seidman. This collection of writings gives information by, about, and for the aged, as well as specific listings of publications, organizations, and services. Among the contributors are Senator Charles Percy, Juanita Kreps, the National Council of Senior Citizens, and the National Caucus on the Black Aged.

You might also enjoy sharing lifestyles and views of five "senior citizens" of children's literature—Dr. Seuss, E. B. White, David McCord, Tillie S. Pine, and Marguerite de Angeli—in Lee Bennett Hopkins' article, "Mother Goose's Sons and Daughters," wherein each discuss their careers, work habits, and their plans for the future.[2]

Making students sensitive to the elderly's feelings, needs, and concerns is an important part of preparing them for their approaching tomorrows. To quote the Gray Panthers' motto, "Age is, after all, the one thing we all share."

REFERENCES[3]

Adler, David A. *A Little At A Time,* illustrated by N. M. Bodecker. Random House, 1976.

Bales, Carol Ann. *Tales of the Elders: A Memory Book of Men and Women Who Came to America as Immigrants, 1900–1930.* Follett, 1977.

Bartoli, Jennifer. *Nonna,* illustrated by Joan E. Drescher. Harvey House, 1975.

Censoni, Robert. *The Shopping-Bag Lady.* Holiday House, 1977.

Gauch, Patricia Lee. *Grandpa and Me,* illustrated by Symeon Shimin. Coward McCann, 1972.

Gross, Ronald, Beatrice Seidman, and Sylvia Seidman, eds. *The New Old: Struggling for Decent Aging.* Anchor Press, 1978.

Skorpen, Liesel Moak. *Mandy's Grandmother,* illustrated by Martha Alexander. Dial, 1975.

Zolotow, Charlotte. *My Grandson Lew,* illustrated by William Pène du Bois. Harper & Row, 1974.

[2]Lee Bennett Hopkins, "Mother Goose's Sons and Daughters," *Teacher* (May/June 1978), pp. 36–38.

[3]See Appendix for publishers' complete addresses.

Coping with life problems

No matter where we teach, we deal with children who must cope with such situations as divorce, death, a handicap, or a lifestyle which differs dramatically from the "average" child's. How can we help these children deal with their conditions and, at the same time, develop positive self-images? How can we sensitize their classmates and nurture healthy attitudes toward differences?

One way is through books that feature young people coping with life's changes and problems. For a troubled child, sometimes just the knowledge that someone else has dealt with a similar situation can be helpful. Before introducing such books, reflect on your students' current and ongoing needs, their abilities to empathize, and so on. This kind of assessment will help you determine when and how you introduce books about life problems and concerns and which books will be appropriate.

VARIED FAMILY SITUATIONS

The volumes discussed below, along with others on similar or related topics, can be placed in a reading area for children to look at independently. If students seem secretive or embarrassed about reading them (and they might), encourage the children to express their responses and externalize feelings about their own problems in a small notebook as a log or diary.

Two anthologies of stories geared toward primary readers that deal with particular children and the life situations they face are *Families Are Like That!* and *Brothers and Sisters Are Like That!*, both compiled by The Child Study Association of America. Each book contains ten carefully chosen stories from acclaimed children's books, including such all-time favorites as *Friday Night Is Papa Night* by Ruth A. Sonneborn (the story of a devoted father who holds two jobs and can see his family only one night a week) and *A Quiet Place* by Rose Blue (about a foster child who finds and then loses his secure quiet place).

The idea that "adoption means belonging" is simply dealt with in *I Am Adopted* by Susan Lapsley. In this small-sized picture book for younger readers, Charles talks about his sister, who is also adopted, their parents, and their life as a family. Three other titles to share with younger readers are *A Look at Adoption* by Margaret Sanford Pursell, with black-and-white photographs by Maria S. Forrai; *The Chosen Baby* by Valentina P. Wasson, illustrated with wash-drawings by Glo Coalson; and *Is That Your Sister?: A True Story About Adoption* by Catherine and Sherry Bunin.

A one-parent family situation is the subject of *I Won't Go Without A Father* by Muriel Stanek, a realistic account of a child's mixed feelings about his one-parent home. The story, also suited to younger readers, revolves around Steve's shame that only his mother will attend an open-house night at school. The reason for the father's absence is left unexplained and open for discussion. Illustrations are by Eleanor Mills.

Sophisticated middle- and upper-graders can explore another kind of single parenthood in Norma Klein's *Mom, the Wolf Man, and Me.* This contemporary offbeat novel tells of 12-year-old Brett, a girl who is glad that her mother had never married and who doesn't mind the state of being fatherless.

Two popular novels of the late 1970s, both for older readers and dealing with foster children, include *The Pinballs* by Betsy Byars, and the 1979 Newbery Honor Book, *The Great Gilly Hopkins* by Katherine Paterson. Both books have received wide critical acclaim and attention.

Death

Introduce primary grade readers to two books by Charlotte Zolotow, an author who has a deep understanding of a child's world. *My Grandson Lew,* illustrated in full color by William

Pène du Bois, is about a child's memories of his deceased grandfather; *A Father Like That,* illustrated by Ben Schecter, tells of a young boy's attempt to imagine what his father, who went away before he was born, might be like.

The subject of death is not new in children's books, and you'll want to dip into both old and modern classics. For example, expose students to the chapter in *Little Women* entitled, "The Valley of the Shadow," in which Louisa May Alcott tenderly treats the death of Beth.

Three Newbery Award-winning titles deal differently with the subject. *Call it Courage,* the 1941 Newbery winner by Armstrong Sperry, relates Mafatu's tragic loss of his mother; *Sounder,* the 1970 Newbery Award winner by William Armstrong, is the touching and memorable story of a black sharecropper family that must bear the heavy sorrows of losing both its father and pet dog; *The Bridge to Terabithia,* the 1978 Newbery Award winner by Katherine Paterson, deals with the relationship between 10-year-olds Jess Aarons and Leslie Burke, two lonely children who invent a kingdom of their own —Terabithia—and Jess' coping with Leslie's accidental drowning.

Should the Children Know?: Encounters with Death in the Lives of Children by Marguerita Rudolph is a resource book for educators and parents. The volume details a teacher's role in helping young boys and girls and their parents understand death when a 4-year-old nursery school classmate dies suddenly of asphyxiation pneumonia. An index is included, as well as a bibliography of children's and adult books and professional articles dealing with the topic.

Divorce

The rising number of separations and divorces will no doubt be felt more frequently in schools. Each year, more than 2.5 million children are faced with the separation or divorce of their parents. Divorce has become so commonplace in the lives of children that when one youngster wrote a fairy tale for his fourth-grade teacher, he ended it by writing, "And so they lived happily together for quite some time!" Many children growing up today don't believe it is very likely that parents can "live happily ever after." Yet, even if divorces and separations are happening to many families, it is still a very painful and jarring experience for each and every individual girl or boy. Often children in such circumstances harbor feelings too personal to share, and the best a teacher can do is to steer them toward books.

For primary-aged readers, *Mommy and Daddy Are Divorced* by Patricia Perry and Marietta Lynch details the new lifestyle and adjustments two young boys have to make living with their mother and seeing their father on periodic visits.

Divorce Is A Grown-Up Problem: A Book About Divorce for Young Children and Their Parents by Janet Sinberg is designed to make things easier for a child caught in the middle and also to waylay the normal fears and insecurities a younger child experiences during this life crisis. The volume is illustrated with black-and-white cartoon illustrations by Nancy Gray.

Middle and upper graders can turn to *What's Going to Happen to Me?: When Parents Separate or Divorce* by Eda Le Shan. This volume, illustrated by Richard Cuffari, provides an excellent direct discussion of the subject, answering the many questions children have before, during, and after the separation of their parents. Part Four of the text focuses on new family combinations for the three out of every four children whose parents remarry. A bibliography is appended listing titles for children 8 through 12, 11 through 14, and for parents' further reading.

Mature readers can consult *How to Get It Together When Your Parents Are Coming Apart* by Arlene Richards and Irene Willis. Like Le Shan's volume, this text realistically deals with the problems youths encounter during the separation process. The last chapter, "Getting Help," provides an excellent guide for troubled teenagers, including names and addresses of social agencies.

Divorce appears in fiction also. The popular and contemporary *My Dad Lives in a Downtown Hotel* by Peggy Mann deals with separation and divorce through the eyes of a young boy. Judy Blume's *It's Not the End of the World* is about a sixth-grader whose parents are on the brink of divorce. Rose Blue's *A Month of Sundays* deals not only with divorce but also with its sensitive repercussions. In this story, a mother and child move from a suburban to an urban setting, and the mother goes to work. Jeffrey must learn to accept his mother's new role and his changed relationship with his father, as well as his own loneliness in a strange environment.

My Other-Mother, My Other-Father by Harriet Langsam Sobol tells of Andrea, a 12-year-old whose parents have divorced and remarried, her feelings about being a stepchild, and the difficulties and advantages of having two sets of parents. Black-and-white photographs by Patricia Agre illustrate this honest, uncompromising look at a situation which is quite familiar to many of today's youth.

Mama by Lee Bennett Hopkins is about a working-class mother who is passionately dedicated to seeing that her two sons (whose father has decamped) have everything they need and want, so she steals. The novel deals with the relationship between the older boy and Mama as he begins to realize that she is stealing. Sheila Schwartz's *Like Mother, Like Me,* a novel for older readers, is a first-person account of Jen, a 16-year-old whose father, an English professor, goes off to Denmark, abandoning her and her devasted mother. Jen witnesses the painful, but often comical, metamorphosis her mother goes through until she finally becomes an independent person.

You might like to encourage parents to borrow some of these titles from classroom, school, or public libraries, as well as acquainting students with them.

If girls and boys do choose to relate their problems openly, you might initiate a daily "magic circle" or meeting time when the class gathers informally to air both school and home problems. An attitude of trust and concern about others can be fostered if judgments are avoided in such open-ended sessions.

THE HANDICAPPED

All students should be helped to cope with feelings about handicapped people, especially now that a majority of states are mainstreaming increasing numbers of handicapped children into regular classrooms. The following titles, just a few of the many dealing with various handicaps, should widen children's attitudes and lead the way to helpful discussions.

He's My Brother, written and illustrated by Joe Lasker, a book for primary graders, deals with a child who suffers feelings of inadequacy because of the "invisible handicap" of a learning disability. The book depicts the tender relationship between the child's parents and sibling and his problems coping with home and school life. *Howie Helps Himself* by Dr. Joan Fassler is a story about a child with cerebral palsy who strives to move his wheelchair by himself. Illustrations are by Joe Lasker.

Handtalk: An ABC of Finger Spelling and Sign Language by Remy Charlip and Mary Beth and George Ancona is the first book of its kind for young people. It details two ways deaf people communicate—finger spelling (forming words letter-by-letter with the fingers of one hand) and signing (making a picture or symbol with one or two hands for each word or idea.) Via this lavishly illustrated text with both black-and-white and full-color photographs, children of all ages are introduced to the language of the deaf. Some might be inspired to create their own signs for nonverbal communication. A note at the end of the book's brief introduction states: "If you want to learn more *Handtalk,* ask a deaf person who knows sign language to show you." A great idea!

Introduce upper-graders to *Don't Feel Sorry for Paul,* written and photographed by Bernard Wolf, also available in Spanish under the title, *No Sientan Lástima por Paul.* Paul is a handicapped boy, whose hands and feet are incompletely formed. With the help of artificial limbs, he can live, play, and work. But like many handicapped individuals, he is sometimes haunted by people who do feel sorry for him, sometimes taunted by people who laugh and cruelly dub him "Captain Hook." Readers of this sensitive, true documentary will find themselves empathizing with Paul.

Feeling Free by Mary Beth Sullivan, Alan J. Brightman, and Joseph Blatt is based on the PBS Award-winning television series and features short stories, games, skits, and activities, all dealing with girls and boys who have a disability. Ginny is a dwarf; John has dyslexia; Gordon is deaf; Hollis has cerebral palsy; Laura is blind. Together with their friends, they explore what it is like to be different, to have a disability, to be noticed, questioned, and stared at. The volume is illustrated with photographs and drawings by Marci Davis and Linda Bourke.

For further reading, suggest that upper-graders consult biographies of such personalities as Helen Keller, Louis Braille, Roy Campanella, and Franklin Delano Roosevelt, famous people who have achieved great goals despite their handicaps.

PHYSICAL AND EMOTIONAL PROBLEMS

Since the introduction of the Education for All Handicapped Children Act of 1975 (Public Law 94–142), mainstreaming has had a widespread impact on students and teachers. There are times, however, when the "well-adjusted" child often has physical or emotional problems that deserve attention and understanding, too. Among such problems are wearing glasses, braces, or hearing aids, and being fat or left-handed. By showing girls and boys through fiction and nonfiction that their "differences" are not always unique and that many other children and adults have learned to cope, you can help them adjust.

Of course, there are many other types of disabilities that confront children. The two professional books listed at the end of this chapter will provide information on other needs.

Seeing Through Any-Color Glasses

Recently, while I was conducting a parent group session, one mother raised a problem she had with her fifth-grade daughter, Karen. A bright, energetic, enthusiastic child, she refused to go to school after being told that she had to wear glasses. "The kids will tease me," and "No one will like me anymore," were some of the comments she uttered day after day, refusing to get "glass eyes" and causing a great deal of confusion and concern within her family. A week after the discussion, our group learned that Karen wasn't really sensitive about the prospect of wearing glasses but was terrified by her peers' horror stories. She heard that "a doctor puts you in a dark room, puts a gigantic machine on your head and drops chemicals in your eyes to see if you are going to become totally blind."

Of course, all children don't go through such anxieties, but many have qualms. Perhaps you can arrange a visit to a local optometrist's or ophthalmologist's office for the class to see exactly what an eye examination consists of. Once they share such an experience and realize that the entire procedure is short and painless, their fears will be overcome.

A charming picture book dealing with visual problems is *Spectacles,* written and illustrated by the popular award-winning author, Ellen Raskin. Iris Fogel sees things other people cannot. For example, one day a fire-breathing dragon knocks at her door; on another, a giant pygmy nuthatch turns up on her front lawn. A closer look reveals them to be Iris's Great-aunt Fanny and her good friend Chester. Obviously the time has come for a visit to the optician. After an initial protest, Iris gets her glasses, realizing now that she can see things *two* ways, an ability that has all kinds of advantages.

What If You Couldn't?

To help a child who is going through a difficult period of adjustment and to make all children sensitive to the disabilities of others, try *What If You Couldn't...?: A Book About Special Needs* by Janet Kamien, illustrated by Signe Hanson. The smooth, easy-to-read text deals with many kinds of problems as well as with feelings and learning disabilities. Throughout the volume, the author encourages readers to imagine they are the person who has the disability and then introduces experiences of how it might feel. For example, Kamien suggests, "To get an idea of what speech reading is like (a technique used by the hearing impaired), say these words while looking in a mirror: *pan, apple, box, shirt, most.* You can see these words all look very different from each other on your lips.

"By studying these differences in school or in a special class, and with lots of practice, you could learn to understand as much as half of what people were saying even if you couldn't hear the words at all."

Help for the Heavy-Hearted

Obesity is a major national health concern. At least one-fourth of all American children suffer from being overweight and too often become easy targets for ridicule and criticism.

A guide for mature readers that emphasizes the complexities of dealing with overweight and the difficulties in achieving weight control is *Fat Free: Common Sense for Young Weight Worriers* by Sara Gilbert. It also includes a scientific explanation of what fat is, an approach to food intake, and suggestions on what children can do about fat. A wealth of information is offered in an appendix, "Where to Find Out More," which includes a bibliography and a list of organizations students can write to for further help.

Several novels for middle-graders about children who have to cope with being fat are *The Planet of Junior Brown* by the Newbery Award winning author, Virginia Hamilton, and *Dinky Hocker Shoots Smack* by M. E. Kerr.

The Teeth of the Matter

If any children in your class are getting braces or perhaps already wear them and have lots of unanswered questions about those metal bands, wires, and elastics, the book to consult is *So You're Getting Braces: A Guide to Orthodontics* by Dr. Alvin Silverstein and Virginia B. Silverstein. The authors explain the process of straightening teeth and include a short history of orthodontics. The volume is liberally illustrated with black-and-white photographs, diagrams, and X-rays of actual cases in progress. An index is included, as well as sources students can write to for additional information.

Younger readers can turn to *You Can't Put Braces on Spaces,* a Greenwillow "Read-Alone" book by Alice Richter and Laura Joffe Numeroff. This humorous tale tells of a young boy who enviously watches his older brother, Neil, being fitted for braces. He wants them, too; however, his two front teeth are missing. Dr. Sherman, the orthodontist, tells him, "You can't put braces on spaces." The book is illustrated in two colors by Numeroff.

On the Other Hand

About one person out of ten, or at least 20 million people in the United States alone, are left-handed, living in a world where common articles and tools—from desks to can openers—are manufactured for the specific use of the right-hand majority. *The Left-Hander's World,* also written by the Silversteins, discusses an "oppressed minority" group that has not received much attention in the past.

The authors give helpful information on serving specific needs, including a list of six mail-order companies that sell products designed for left-handers. A brief chapter, "Famous Left-Handers," covers such notables as Michelangelo, Leonardo da Vinci, Ringo Starr, Paul McCartney, Mark Spitz, and astronaut Wally Schirra. The book is illustrated with black-and-white photographs and includes an index.

A good resource for additional information and moral support is Lefthanders International, which publishes *Lefty,* a quarterly magazine, and a LEFTYletter, an eight-times-a-year newsletter. Write to the association at 3601 S. W. 29th Street, Topeka, Kansas 66614, for membership information.

FOR THE PROFESSIONAL SHELF

The Bookfinder: A Guide to Children's Literature About the Needs and Problems of Youth Aged 2–15, compiled by Sharon

Spredemann Dreyer, can lead you to many other titles and subject areas dealing with life-coping. Annotations of over 1000 books covering more than 450 topics of concern to today's young readers appear herein, giving complete bibliographic information, main subject headings, synopses, reading levels, and related print and nonprint media including films, tapes, and materials for the blind or the physically handicapped. Topics from abandonment to worries are all cross-referenced. The volume is published in a split format; the top section includes indices of subjects, authors, titles, and a publisher's directory; the bottom half contains the annotations.

Another reference volume is *Notes from a Different Drummer: A Guide to Juvenile Fiction Portraying the Handicapped* by Barbara H. Baskin and Karen H. Harris. This book includes chapters on "Society and the Handicapped," "Literary Treatment of Disability," "Assessing and Using Juvenile Fiction Portraying the Disabled," and "Patterns and Trends in Juvenile Fiction, 1940–1975." The bulk of the text features "An Annotated Guide to Juvenile Fiction Portraying the Handicapped, 1940–1975." Title and subject indices are appended.

REFERENCES[1]

Alcott, Louisa May. *Little Women.* Available in many hardcover and paperback editions.

Armstrong, William. *Sounder.* Harper & Row, 1969; available in paperback.

Baskin, Barbara H., and Karen H. Harris. *Notes from A Different Drummer.* Bowker, 1977.

Blue, Rose. *A Month of Sundays.* Watts, 1972.

Blume, Judy. *It's Not the End of the World.* Bradbury, 1972; Dell paperback.

Bunin, Catherine and Sherry. *Is That Your Sister? A True Story About Adoption.* Pantheon, 1976.

Byars, Betsy. *The Pinballs.* Harper & Row, 1977; also available in paperback.

Charlip, Remy, Mary Beth, and George Ancona. *Hand-talk: An ABC of Finger Spelling and Sign Language.* Parents' Magazine Press, 1974.

The Child Study Association of America, compilers. *Brothers and Sisters Are Like That!* Crowell, 1971.

———. *Families Are Like That!* Crowell, 1975.

[1]See Appendix for publishers' complete addresses.

Dreyer, Sharon Spredemann. *The Bookfinder: A Guide to Children's Literature About the Needs and Problems of Youth Aged 2–15.* American Guidance, 1978.

Fassler, Joan. *Howie Helps Himself.* Whitman, 1975.

Gilbert, Sara. *Fat Free: Common Sense for Young Weight Worriers.* Macmillan, 1975; Collier paperback.

Hamilton, Virginia. *The Planet of Junior Brown.* Macmillan, 1971; also available in paperback.

Hopkins, Lee Bennett. *Mama.* Knopf, 1977; Dell paperback.

Kamien, Janet. *What If You Couldn't . . .?: A Book About Special Needs.* Scribner, 1979.

Kerr, M. E. *Dinky Hocker Shoots Smack.* Harper & Row, 1972; Dell paperback.

Klein, Norma. *Mom, The Wolf Man, and Me.* Pantheon, 1972; Avon paperback.

Lapsley, Susan. *I Am Adopted.* Bradbury, 1975.

Lasker, Joe. *He's My Brother.* Whitman, 1974.

Le Shan, Eda. *What's Going to Happen to Me?: When Parents Separate or Divorce.* Four Winds, 1978.

Mann, Peggy. *My Dad Lives in a Downtown Hotel.* Doubleday, 1973; Avon paperback.

Paterson, Katherine. *The Bridge to Terabithia.* Crowell, 1978; Avon paperback.

————. *The Great Gilly Hopkins.* Crowell, 1978; Avon paperback.

Perry, Patricia, and Marietta Lynch. *Mommy and Daddy Are Divorced.* Dial, 1978.

Pursell, Margaret Sanford. *A Look at Adoption.* Lerner, 1978.

Raskin, Ellen. *Spectacles.* Atheneum, 1978; also available in paperback.

Richards, Arlene, and Irene Willis. *How to Get It Together When Your Parents Are Coming Apart.* McKay, 1976; Bantam paperback.

Richter, Alice, and Laura Joffe Numeroff. *You Can't Put Braces on Spaces.* Greenwillow, 1979.

Rudolph, Marguerita. *Should the Children Know? Encounters with Death in the Lives of Children.* Schocken, 1978.

Schwartz, Shelia. *Like Mother, Like Me.* Pantheon, 1978; Bantam paperback.

Silverstein, Dr. Alvin, and Virginia B. Silverstein. *The Left-Hander's World.* Follett, 1977.

————. *So You're Getting Braces: A Guide to Orthodontics.* Lippincott, 1977; also available in paperback.

Sinberg, Janet. *Divorce Is A Grown-Up Problem: A Book About Divorce for Young Children and Their Parents.* Avon paperback.

Sobol, Harriet Langsam. *My Other-Mother, My Other-Father.* Macmillan, 1979.

Sperry, Armstrong. *Call It Courage.* Macmillan, 1940; Scholastic paperback.

Stanek, Muriel. *I Won't Go Without A Father.* Whitman, 1972.
Sullivan, Mary Beth, Alan J. Brightman, and Joseph Blatt. *Feeling Free.* Addison-Wesley, 1979; also available in paperback.
Wasson, Valentina P. *The Chosen Baby.* Lippincott, 1977.
Wolf, Bernard. *Don't Feel Sorry for Paul.* Lippincott, 1974.
———. *No Sientan Lástima por Paul.* Lippincott, 1979.
Zolotow, Charlotte. *A Father Like That.* Harper & Row, 1971.
———. *My Grandson Lew.* Harper & Row, 1974.

"Democracy is not a spectator sport!"

Democracy—what does the word mean to the students in your class? Using the slogan "Democracy Is Not a Spectator Sport!" from a television announcement for the League of Women Voters in Connecticut might provide the incentive to involve children in reading and learning about the multifaceted ways in which our country is governed. To begin, you might pose questions such as: What do you think a democracy is? What is a government? What types of governments do other areas of the world have? What forms of government do your city and state have?

The First Book of Local Government by James A. Eichner reveals how government works below the federal level. Similarities in the various forms of city and county government are outlined, and the functions of city governments, such as public utilities, are explained. This book points out to children that few American communities are run exactly the same way and that location, history, population, size, and geography contribute to the makeup of various kinds of local government. A glossary and index are appended. Black-and-white illustrations are by Dan Nevins.

LET YOUR FINGERS DO THE WALKING

To show students which departments, agencies, and offices carry out the laws in their area, ask them to bring in local telephone directories or your state's manual, also known as a register. It will be helpful to first discuss the similarities and differences between the directory or manual and more familiar reference books such as the dictionary and encyclopedia.

What government agencies are listed in the telephone book? Many directories categorize agencies under federal, state, county, city, town, and/or village divisions. Can the students explain how each of these designations is different? What does each mean? What type of place do you live in? What do you think each agency listed is responsible for? A quick look will unveil some unusual government posts that the children might not know exist—from the County Executive Office of Manpower Planning to the Sealer Weights and Measures Office.

Several pages in *The First Book of Local Government* briefly discuss jobs in local government. Heighten children's career awareness by having the class write invitations to people who work for government agencies, asking them to come into the classroom to discuss their job roles and how they trained for them.

GOVERNMENT AT WORK

As the children become familiar with the various agencies, plan a walk around the neighborhood to see government at work on a daily basis. During the stroll, encourage them to write down examples of government services that relate to their community.

Prepare a chart with columns labeled *federal, state, county, city,* and *village.* Using the data they have gathered, have them list which divisions of government are responsible for such services as the installation of sewers and traffic lights, mail delivery, placement of mailboxes, issuing license plates and dog licenses, garbage disposal, police and fire protection, education, and libraries.

Middle-grade readers can learn a great deal about the workings of the senate in *I Want to Know About the Senate* by Senator Charles Percy of Illinois. Based on questions asked by girls and boys from around the country, Percy tells how he got into politics, describes a normal work day, explains the workings of the government—particularly the legislative branch—and discusses some of his special concerns. Illustrated with black-and-white photographs, this is a lively introduction to the United States Senate.

Poll the class to find out if they know who their state senators are. If they do not know, the time will be ripe to acquaint them with these individuals, perhaps writing to their offices for background information on their lives and work.

Another fact-filled volume to share about government workers is *The President's Cabinet and How It Grew,* written and illustrated by Nancy Winslow Parker. The appealing and accessible picture-book format tells readers how this group of presidential advisors came into being and grew in importance during our history. The president's cabinet is traced from the first four advisors who served President George Washington in 1789, to the twelve men and women in President Jimmy Carter's cabinet, including the new secretary of energy.

IT'S THE LAW

America is governed by many laws. What is a law? How does it become part of the American scene? How are laws enforced? Why are new laws made? Why are laws changed? Although these questions are complicated, they can be discussed with students of all ages.

The humorous tale of *Shiver, Gobble and Snore: The Story About Why People Need Laws* by Marie Winn and illustrated by Whitney Darrow, Jr., can help even the youngest reader begin to understand the importance of rules and regulations. Shiver, Gobble, and Snore are tired of their country and feel particularly downtrodden under a king who makes rules for everything. In their country, "There were rules about candy and rules about cakes. Rules about spiders and rules about snakes. . . . There were rules about tulips and rules about roses. Rules about eyebrows and rules about noses." When the three protagonists trek to a land where there are no rules at all, chaos reigns. Reluctantly, they admit that a few rules are necessary for people to live together peacefully. In the back of the book, Winn offers suggestions to parents and teachers on children's activities that reinforce the book's theme. These include a game about laws, skits for dramatic play, and places to visit.

"Rules of the Game," the first chapter in *Leaders, Laws and Citizens: The Story of Democracy and Government* by William Wise, illustrated by Mila Lazarevich, makes lawmaking a group endeavor. Included are questions to ponder on the necessity of rules at home, such as: What are some special rules in your own family? Are there any you dislike, because they seem unfair? Can you ever dislike a rule that *is* fair? To stir up classroom dialogue on this subject, ask the students how they would run their future families. You might want to share some of your own childhood experiences and compare notes on family rules and regulations.

The volume goes on to give a history of American government, emphasizing the democracy of our system. Difficult-to-explain concepts—balance of power, the division of federal income—are simply and clearly defined. This is a good choice to read aloud to young children or to offer to middle-graders as a basis for further discussion.

American Freedom and the Bill of Rights, also by Wise, succinctly deals with rights, from the Declaration of Independence to equal opportunities for women. Subjects include America's problems in its formative stages, how and why certain laws were enacted, and the amendment process, with particular emphasis on the first ten amendments, the Bill of Rights. Some of today's legal controversies that are covered in the book—the limits of free speech, gun control, and wiretapping—offer intermediate-grade girls and boys opportunity to examine current affairs. Illustrations are by Roland Rodegast.

Informative and giggle-provoking for children of all ages is *You Can't Eat Peanuts in Church and Other Little Known Laws,* written and illustrated by Barbara Seulig. This easy-to-read small volume is a joyous collection celebrating many of the strange and amusing laws that have gone into effect in American history. Children may find that some of the laws had been set forth in their very own city and state. For example, in Hawaii it is illegal to insert pennies in your ears; it is against the law for a donkey to sleep in a bathtub in Brooklyn, New York; and owning a dog more than 10 inches high was once banned in Boston. Promote some research on the topic by encouraging the students to write to local or state officials to find out if such laws still exist or have been repealed and why they were passed in the first place. Interested students might delve into peculiar laws in their own communities or research the history of recently instituted laws. By the way, you can't eat peanuts in church in the state of Massachusetts!

Mature upper-graders can glean a great deal from *A Guide to the Supreme Court* by Dorothy A. Marquardt. Part One of the text discusses the function and history of the Supreme Court, its purpose and authority, and its daily routine, and offers in-depth profiles on the men whose decisions have helped shape our nation. Illustrated with black-and-white photographs, the book also includes the complete text of the Constitution of the United States, a glossary of legal terms, a summary of the Court's landmark descisions from 1873–1976, a bibliography, and an index.

MULTIMEDIA

Foundations of Justice, produced by Charles E. Merrill Company, is a multimedia program for use in upper-grade classrooms. It is designed to aid students' understanding of the basic concepts on which our system of justice is built. Four full-color sound filmstrips in cartoon format are contained within the kit, including "The Battle of Oog and Ugh: The Adversary Process" in which two cavemen argue over who owns Snagglefang, a sabertoothed tiger. To settle the matter, the people of the village eventually set up a courtroom with judicial rules to protect the rights of all parties involved. Other components of the package are a teacher's guide and student activity booklets that encourage role playing, mock trials, case studies, values-clarification activities, and vocabulary reinforcement. For additional information write to the company for a descriptive brochure.

Whether it is a class rule, a city ordinance, or a constitutional amendment, all citizens—regardless of age—must be active participants in a democracy. It is the only way to keep it from being a spectator sport!

REFERENCES[1]

Eichner, James A. *The First Book of Local Government.* Watts, 1976.
Marquardt, Dorothy A. *A Guide to the Supreme Court.* Bobbs-Merrill, 1977.
Percy, Charles. *I Want to Know About the Senate.* Doubleday, 1976.
Parker, Nancy Winslow. *The President's Cabinet and How It Grew.* Parent's Magazine Press, 1978.
Seulig, Barbara. *You Can't Eat Peanuts in Church and Other Little Known Laws.* Doubleday, 1975.

[1]See Appendix for publishers' complete addresses.

Winn, Marie. *Shiver, Gobble and Snore: The Story About Why People Need Laws.* Simon & Schuster, 1971.

Wise, William. *American Freedom and the Bill of Rights.* Parent's Magazine Press, 1975.

———. *Leaders, Laws and Citizens: The Story of Democracy and Government.* Parent's Magazine Press, 1972.

6

Dollars and sense:
Learning about money

Most children learn at an early age that they must exchange coins and bills for goods and services. What they may not know is how money developed historically and how it functions in our society. The following titles and activities, as well as your own social studies and mathematics lessons, not only can help children become more knowledgeable about but also can show them how to earn, spend, and save it regularly.

WHAT IS MONEY?

A fact hunt is one way to uncover a variety of money-related topics for later study. Ask students to search for one or two particulars about money (such as the average American's yearly earnings), write them down on slips of paper, and share them with classmates, perhaps via a bulletin board display.

Girls and boys of all ages will be fascinated to know that they can uncode paper bills. Inside a small black circle on the left front side, directly above the green serial number, a letter appears denoting what city the money comes from. If children look more closely at the circle, they will also see the city and state of one of the twelve Federal Reserve Banks that are in charge of putting money into circulation.

All paper money is printed in Washington, D.C., by the Bureau of Printing and Engraving, part of the United States Treasury Department. From Washington, the money is sent to a Federal Reserve Bank. Here is a list of the twelve cities and states where Federal Reserve Banks are located, along with their letter codes:

Boston, Massachusetts	A
New York, New York	B
Philadelphia, Pennsylvania	C
Cleveland, Ohio	D
Richmond, Virginia	E
Atlanta, Georgia	F
Chicago, Illinois	G
St. Louis, Missouri	H
Minneapolis, Minnesota	I
Kansas City, Kansas	J
Dallas, Texas	K
San Francisco, California	L

Encourage students to check a few dollar bills. Some may have traveled from cities quite far away from where they live. Discuss with students how they might have reached their hometown.

An excellent place for younger readers to begin a search for money facts is *Money, Money, Money* by Ruth Belov Gross, with collage drawings by Leslie Jacobs. This brief, lively text consists of a host of questions and answers on such subjects as how money was invented, how it has changed through the years, how paper currency originated, and the role it has played in our history.

Mature readers can dip into *A Matter of Money: What Do You Do With A Dollar?* by Ruth Cavin, which covers the history of the United States monetary system, taxes, and credit, among other topics. Also included are a glossary, an index, and a list of books to further explore these topics.

HOW TO EARN MONEY

Spending money usually means having to earn it first. How many ways do your students know to put some change in their pockets? If their ideas are limited to a traditional few—delivering papers, baby-sitting, mowing lawns—they will welcome the host of paying possibilities described in the two titles below.

Good Cents: Every Kid's Guide to Making Money by members of the Amazing Life Games Company, with black-and-white illustrations by Martha Hairston and James Robertson, is divided into four sections: "Weekenders," "Any Timers," "Special Timers," and "Summer Timers," giving students step-by-step guidelines for getting into a wide variety of minibusinesses. A brief concluding chapter, "You and Your Money," provides information on what to do with accumulated earnings.

Upper-graders can find 35 job roles devised *by* young people throughout the country in *Dozens of Ways to Make Money* by Yvonne Michie Horn. A wide variety of jobs are included, from selling dried weeds arranged into bunches of "decorative grasses" to umpiring various sports events. Throughout the volume, practical tips are given on sound businesslike procedures, costs and methods of operation and pricing, and advertising and selling products or services. The last chapter, "Tips on Advertising," shows readers how to design posters, fliers, and business cards.

HOW MONEY MOVES

Most children do not earn enough money to pay income taxes. However, since every April 15 marks our national tax return deadline, it would be interesting to discuss with children the *modus operandi* of the federal and state tax system. Browsing through blank tax forms with your students is a good introduction to the vocabulary, tables, and computations involved. The forms are usually available at the local post office or Internal Revenue Service office. For assistance in answering questions the children raise about the forms, consider inviting a tax consultant to class. His or her explanations will help students better understand how tax rates are determined and why they hear adults groan on or before April 15!

Another aspect of taxes children can explore is Social Security, beginning with applying for their own cards. All a student has to do is complete and mail in a simple form (consult the local telephone directory under "United States Government Services" for the nearest Social Security Administration Office to obtain forms), accompanied, in most cases, by a copy of his or her birth certificate. Prior to this fill-in-the-blank activity, you might invite a guest speaker from the local office to discuss the system, explaining what that lifelong number is all about.

The discipline of saving money and the pleasure of watching

it grow and earn interest are only two aspects of banking. In addition to asking local bank personnel to talk to your students about how banks operate, refer them to these three excellent sources of information. By the way, the books can also motivate readers to further study career opportunities in the field.

Money, Money, Money: How To Get and Keep It by Tom Morgan simply explains such things as bank interest, stocks, profits, bonds, mortgages, and bankruptcy. Line drawings are by Joe Ciardiello. The easy-to-understand language and illustrations in *The Money Movers: What Banks Do and Why* by Don Colen clarifies such complexities as where money comes from, how it moves around, and where it goes. A final chapter tells of future changes in the way we might use money and the ways banks work. A glossary is included.

Twenty-three personal on-the-job interviews with men and women are the focus of *Banking, Money and Finance* by April Klimley, part of the "Here is Your Career" series published by G. P. Putnam's Sons. Traditional career choices are related, as well as new occupations opening up in such areas as marketing, computer programming, and electronic banking. The volume, illustrated in black-and-white photographs, contains a glossary and an index.

THE UPS AND DOWNS OF ECONOMICS

Budding entrepreneurs or other children interested in how goods and services are produced, distributed, and consumed will enjoy reading *How To Turn Lemons Into Money: A Child's Guide to Economics* and *How To Turn Up Into Down Into Up: A Child's Guide to Inflation, Depression and Economics Recovery* by Louise Armstrong, both illustrated by cartoonist Bill Basso.

In *How To Turn Lemons...*, a whirlwind course in economics is represented by a young girl who sets up a lemonade stand. Her business moves on from the basics—fruit, water, and sugar—to deal with the more complex concepts of market value, original investment, labor, strikes, boycotts, and diminishing profits. *How To Turn Up...* continues the pleasures and frustrations of lemonade-stand ownership, taking readers further into the intricacies of private enterprise.

A third volume, *A Kid's Guide to the Economy* by Manfred G. Riedel, contains 27 short anecdotes about boys and girls learning about capitalism, competition, zero growth, and oligopoly (a few producers controlling a specific market). The volume, illustrated in black-and-while cartoon drawings by Ric Estrada, includes an index.

Helping children acquire "money sense" is one of the essential survival skills. But as these books and ideas demonstrate, it can also be a fascinating exploration of institutions, concepts, and systems basic to modern life.

MONEY IN FICTION

Middle-grade readers might look for and discuss novels dealing with money and business. The four titles below are popular choices among girls and boys.

Jean Merrill's *The Toothpaste Millionaire* is a delightful romp about Rufus, a black boy, who challenges the entire business community by marketing, and making a fortune, from a product which he simply calls "toothpaste!" *Alvin's Swap Shop* by Clifford B. Hicks, with black-and-white illustrations by Bill Sobol, features Alvin, the Magic Brain, who trades up from an ant collection to a well-appointed gasoline station swap-center. In the process, he helps capture a criminal seeking a rare stamp.

Hawkins by Barbara Brooks Wallace deals with Harvey Small, a perennial contest-enterer who wins, of all things, a gentlemen's gentleman, Hawkins. Harvey, with Hawkins' help, proceeds to enter the world of money and punch stands. Black-and-white illustrations are by Gloria Kamen. In *100 Pounds of Popcorn* by Hazel Krantz, Andy Taylor is catapulted into the world of business when he receives 100 pounds of popcorn. Finding places to dispose of the popcorn teaches Andy and his friends a great deal about the law of supply and demand. Black-and-white pictures are by Charles Geer.

REFERENCES[1]

The Amazing Life Games Company. *Good Cents: Every Kid's Guide to Making Money.* Houghton Mifflin, 1974.
Armstrong, Louise. *How To Turn Lemons Into Money: A Child's Guide to Economics.* Harcourt, 1977; also available in paperback.

[1]See Appendix for publishers' complete addresses.

————. *How To Turn Up Into Down Into Up: A Child's Guide to Infla-tion, Depression and Economics Recovery.* Harcourt, 1978; also available in paperback.

Cavin, Ruth. *A Matter of Money: What Do You Do with a Dollar?* S. G. Phillips, 1978.

Colen, Dan. *The Money Movers: What Banks Do and Why.* McKay, 1978.

Gross, Ruth Belov. *Money, Money, Money.* Scholastic paperback.

Hicks, Clifford B. *Alvin's Swap Shop.* Holt, Rinehart and Winston, 1976; Scholastic paperback.

Horn, Yvonne Michie. *Dozens of Ways to Make Money.* Harcourt, 1978; also available in paperback.

Klimley, April. *Banking, Money and Finance.* Putnam, 1978.

Krantz, Hazel. *100 Pounds of Popcorn.* Vanguard, 1961.

Merrill, Jean. *The Toothpaste Millionaire.* Houghton Mifflin, 1974.

Morgan, Tom. *Money, Money, Money: How to Get and Keep It.* Putnam, 1978.

Riedel, Manfred G. *A Kid's Guide to the Economy.* Prentice-Hall, 1978.

Wallace, Barbara Brooks. *Hawkins.* Abingdon, 1977; Scholastic paperback under the title *The Contest Kid.*

7

Everybody has a body!

Puzzles, enigmas, and mysteries present themselves whenever teachers and students undertake a study of the human body, one of nature's most unique "machines." By using a wide variety of nonfiction books and a few human resources, you can start some fascinating classroom fact-finding and lead children to a lifelong interest in the intricacies of physical growth, development, and functions.

After boys and girls have perused a variety of books relating to the human body, plan a project on human biology and health. You might want to start with the help of the school nurse or a local doctor. Before inviting them into class, poll the students to find out what questions and concerns they would like discussed.

How We Are Born, How We Grow, How Our Bodies Work ... And How We Learn, written and illustrated by Joe Kaufman, contains a treasure lode of information for children of all ages. An attractive, oversized volume designed to give girls and boys a true understanding of their bodies, it answers many questions children might pose. For example: What makes you yawn when you are sleepy? Where do tears come from? Why does your body shiver when you are cold? Colorful illustrations help illuminate human processes such as birth, sight, digestion, dreaming, learning, and memory. Younger students will glean a great deal just by thumbing through the pages; older students can use the text for reference.

To give children an inside look at their insides, have them study some X-ray photographs. To obtain these films, enlist the assistance of your school's nurse in contacting a local hospital, radiologist, dentist, doctor, or the public relations department of a medical school. Tape the films to a sun-filled window and have the children locate bones and organs.

Bodies by Barbara Brenner is designed for preschoolers and primary-age children. The simple text and excellent black-and-white photographs by George Ancona explore what fun it is to have a body—one that is uniquely yours!

The "Let's-Read-And-Find-Out Science Books" series published by Thomas Y. Crowell includes 19 titles, each dealing with a specific body part. The easy-to-read content and profuse illustrations are inviting to younger children and intriguing to middle- and upper-graders on their way to further research.[1]

A Drop of Blood by Paul Showers, illustrated in color by Don Madden, one of the titles in this series, explains what blood is, how it works for our bodies, and why it is important to us. After introducing this title, arrange for each child in the class to have his or her blood type determined by a nurse or doctor. This simple process only takes seconds, and knowing what blood type one has can be of utmost importance. By looking at the small samples, children will quickly see that everybody's blood looks alike, even though there are four different groups—A, B, AB, and O. Each contains a slightly different chemical makeup in the blood cells. Some have an extra A substance, and some a B, some A and B, and some have no extra substance (O). When everybody's blood type is identified, prepare a class chart listing the children's names and their blood types. Then have each child prepare a card cut from oaktag or cardboard that notes their blood type, name, address, and telephone number. If possible, laminate the cards for durability. This personal document can be carried in pockets or wallets.

Other titles in the Crowell science book series will lead to many experiments and activities. For example, another book by Showers, *Your Skin and Mine*, encourages readers to make and examine fingerprints. The text, illustrated by Paul Galdone, is also available in Spanish, *Tu Piel y la Mía*. In *Straight Hair, Curly Hair* by Augusta Goldin, illustrated by Ed Ember-

---

[1]For a complete listing of titles, write to the publishing company requesting a catalog in care of Juvenile Books Promotion.

ley, two easy experiments demonstrate the strength and elasticity of hair. This, too, is published in Spanish, titled *Pelo Lacio, Pelo Rizo*. Many of the other titles are available in Spanish language editions, as well as paperback and sound-filmstrip sets.

BREAKS AND BRUISES

Unfortunately, sometimes body parts break down. Few children go through life without the pain of some disorder or other. The world of children's books can't heal wounds, but it can offer helpful first-aid solutions.

Ouch! All About Cuts and Hurts by Rita Golden Gelman and Susan Kovacs Buxbaum is a simple introduction to what happens to the body when common injuries occur such as black-and-blue marks, bumps, cuts, nosebleeds, stitches, and scars, and how the body reacts to repair such damages. The volume, organized alphabetically, is illustrated in cartoon-like drawings by Jan Pyk. *The Fall Down, Break A Bone, Skin Your Knee Book*, written and illustrated by Kathleen Elgin, explains the physical reactions that take place when the body combats injuries and illnesses such as burns, skinned knees, warts, sunburns, and infectious diseases. A short section devoted to first aid is also included.

Brief, humorous stories on how to administer first aid for 26 common household accidents compose the antidotal *What To Do When There's No One But You* by Harriet Gore, a professional nurse. Step-by-step instructions illustrated by David Lindroth are given for treating nasty "oopses," such as knife cuts, scrapes, and burns, and some common "ouches" like poison ivy and sunburn. Keep this handy at home and at school, preferably near a first-aid kit or medicine chest.

These titles can lead to discussions and demonstrations of what first aid is, what items should be contained in a kit or home medicine chest, the purpose of each, and directions for their application. Remind all children, especially younger ones, that medicine chest items are not playthings and that they should never experiment with any medicines or pills. Small-group visits to the nurse's office might be arranged to display and explain the contents of a typical first-aid kit and to find out what should fill home medicine cabinet shelves.

IN SICKNESS AND IN HEALTH

Being sick is a bore! But knowing just *why* you are sick can sometimes make you feel a wee bit better.

The Sick Book: Questions and Answers About Hiccups and Mumps, Sneezes and Bumps, and Other Things That Go Wrong With Us by Marie Winn is an informative volume about common childhood illnesses. Presented in a lively question-and-answer format, the various sections deal with colds and flus, allergies, chicken pox, mumps and measles, skin troubles, and broken bones. Each ailment is presented so that readers will understand what happens when they are sick. A special section at the end of the book explains how our bodies work when they are healthy. Whimsical drawings by Fred Brenner offer healing humor. Who can resist a giraffe with a sore neck, a bear with a runny nose, or a camel with a stitched hump?

Germs Make Me Sick: A Health Handbook for Kids by Parnell Donahue and Helen Capellaro describes a wide variety of diseases and their treatment, and a brief discussion of germs in general. Included are diseases of the gastrointestinal tract (mumps, food poisoning, stomach-sickness), the respiratory tract (colds, sore throats, sinusitus), germs on the skin (warts, acne, athlete's foot), and viral exanthems (measles, chicken pox). A separate chapter discusses "Some Diseases You Probably Won't Get," such as meningitis, rabies, and rheumatic fever. The final chapter tells about "Getting Well and Staying There." A glossary and index are appended. Black-and-white illustrations are by Kelly Oechsli.

If any of your children sneeze every August, get those annoying itchy bumps on their skin when they eat chocolate, or have trouble breathing when they play with a puppy, *Itch, Sniffle and Sneeze: All About Asthma, Hay Fever and other Allergies* by Dr. Alvin Silverstein and Virginia B. Silverstein is a book to pass along to them. The text succinctly tells what allergies are, how the body reacts to them, things people are allergic to, and how to cope with allergies. Two-color illustrations are by Roy Doty.

A cheery note from classmates and the loan of *The Pooh Get-Well Book: Recipes and Activities to Help You Recover from Wheezles and Sneezles* by Virginia H. Ellison will brighten the gloom of any absentee. Puzzles, poems, word fun, things to eat and drink to provide strength, and things to make and play while recovering are all here. The book is embellished with quotations and drawings from the original "Pooh" books by A. A. Milne and Ernest H. Shepard.

Much of the fear of being ill lies in the unknown. The mere thought of hospitals, ambulances, and medical instruments can be upsetting for many children. But two communities have devised unique approaches that help alleviate these fears. You may want to consider similar programs for your students. In a Northampton, Massachusetts, program developed and run by Mariann Stackpole (an early education specialist), 3- to 8-year-olds visit Cooley Dickinson Hospital to learn what a hospital is and what its workers do. The youngsters also listen to one another's heartbeats with a stethoscope, see how blood pressure is measured and, more important, ask questions to air any hospital fears they might have. In Scarsdale, New York, and Fair Lawn, New Jersey, some primary-grade teachers annually invite the local volunteer ambulance corps to school to give children the opportunity to see the inside of this kind of vehicle and learn how it saves lives.

If a trip to the hospital—as visitor or patient—is scheduled for your students, two fiction selections for younger readers will help smooth the way. In *Curious George Goes to the Hospital*, written and illustrated by Margaret and H. A. Rey, the all-time favorite chimp swallows a piece of a jigsaw puzzle and is hospitalized after an X-ray reveals the cause of his discomfort. Marjorie Weinman Sharmat's *I Want Mama* tenderly describes a young girl's concern over her mother going to the hospital. The expressive illustrations by Emily Arnold McCully enhance this reassuring story.

When new vocabulary pops up, steer older readers to *Medical Talk for Beginners* by Dr. Robert H. Curtis, an attractively designed dictionary of medical terms from *abdomen* to *X-ray*, illustrated with black-and-white drawings by William Jaber.

Reading, research, and learning activities can lead to increased career awareness for older girls and boys. The medical field offers many job opportunities that students might not be aware of. Encourage them to look through want ads in local newspapers to find out what kinds of health-care jobs are available in their community. Several students could prepare reports or interviews on job roles of specialized types of doctors such as pediatricians, internists, anesthesiologists, as well as physical and occupational interests.

Everybody has a body. But learning how and why it works means healthier and happy everybodys!

REFERENCES[2]

Brenner, Barbara. *Bodies*. Dutton, 1973.

Curtis, Dr. Robert H. *Medical Talk for Beginners*. Messner, 1976.

Donahue, Parnell, and Helen Capellaro. *Germs Make Me Sick: A Health Handbook for Kids*. Knopf, 1975; also available in paperback.

Elgin, Kathleen. *The Fall Down, Break A Bone, Skin Your Knee Book*. Walker, 1975

Ellison, Virginia H. *The Pooh Get-Well Book: Recipes and Activities to Help You Recover from Wheezles and Sneezles*. Dutton, 1973; Dell paperback.

Gelman, Rita Golden, and Susan Kovacs Buxbaum. *Ouch! All About Cuts and Hurts.* Harcourt, 1977.

Golden, Augusta. *Pela Lacio, Pelo Rizo*. Crowell, 1966; also available in paperback.

———. *Straight Hair, Curly Hair*. Crowell, 1966; also available in paperback.

Gore, Harriet. *What to Do When There's No One But You*. Prentice-Hall, 1974.

Kaufman, Joe. *How We Are Born, How We Grow, How Our Bodies Work . . . and How We Learn*. Western, 1975.

Rey, Margaret, and H. A. Rey *Curious George Goes to the Hospital*. Houghton Mifflin, 1966; also available in paperback.

Sharmat, Marjorie Weinmann. *I Want Mama*. Harper & Row, 1974.

Showers, Paul. *A Drop of Blood*. Crowell, 1967; also available in paperback.

———. *Tu Piel y la Mía*. Crowell, 1965; also available in paperback.

———. *Your Skin and Mine*. Crowell, 1965; also available in paperback.

Silverstein, Dr. Alvin, and Virginia B. Silverstein. *Itch, Sniffle and Sneeze: All About Asthma, Hay Fever and other Allergies*. Four Winds, 1978

Winn, Marie. *The Sick Book: Questions and Answers About Hiccups and Mumps, Sneezes and Bumps, and other Things That Go Wrong With Us.* Four Winds, 1976.

[2]See Appendix for publishers' complete addresses.

Family roots

Since the publication and broadcasts of Alex Haley's *Roots* and "Roots: The Next Generations," genealogical libraries have been filled with Americans of all ages who are delving into records to find their family histories. For example, at the National Archives in Washington, D.C., the center for government historical documents, the number of visitors has risen by as much as 500 people per week.

In the article, "The Great Ancestor Hunt," Harriet Van Horne, a well-known essayist, stated:

> Today, astonishingly, genealogy is the third-ranking American hobby. And it's being pursued with typically American avidity. Climbing the family tree rates right after stamp- and coin-collecting. Libraries, town halls and old cemeteries are under virtual siege by the new breed of genealogists. A recent Gallup poll showed 69 percent of us are eager to know more about our ancestors. As social changes go, this one is unprecedented; a mere decade ago it was bad form even to mention one's ancestors.[1]

Tapping the interest in the classroom can lead to many research projects and activities such as map work (plotting a class or school's population or origins on a world or United States map), creative writing (putting together diaries of past lives and experiences), dramatics (reenacting scenes from a

[1] *Family Weekly,* July 10, 1977, page 7.

family's history), and oral language presentations (interviewing and reporting findings).

START WITH THE PRESENT

"My family history begins with me," stated Iphicrates, a shoemaker's son who became a general in ancient Greece, and this quote illustrates an important point about investigating the personalized past. Before children can glean, interpret, and learn from their histories, they must know something about their present selves.

Two professional texts that will give you hundreds of tried-and-tested ideas to bolster a child's self-concept are *Let Them Be Themselves: Language Arts for Children in Elementary Schools* by Lee Bennett Hopkins, and *100 Ways to Enhance Self-Concept in the Classroom: A Handbook for Teachers and Parents* by Jack Canfield and Harold C. Wells. The first chapter of *Let Them Be Themselves* cites ideas and examples of projects carried out in developing children's positive concepts about their cultural and racial backgrounds. The remainder of the text stresses self-concept through children's literature and creative writing, oral language, and critical thinking activities. Appendices include selected book lists for use with all grade levels. *100 Ways . . .* is an easy-to-read text that is chockfull of ideas on such topics as personality strengths, accepting one's body, and relationships with others.

WHEN DID YOU ARRIVE?

Immigrants to the new world, settlers of the West, and movers from the country to the cities and suburbs are three kinds of "new arrivals" children may encounter in their pasts. To highlight their own debuts into the world, plan a birth certificate bulletin board display with the class. Ask parents to send in copies of children's birth records, since originals may get lost or damaged "in transit." Then, mount them on colored paper and arrange them attractively. A great deal can be learned from this document, such as complete family names, birth dates, and time and place of birth. After the children have discussed the documents, they can begin to dig into other records with the family's help. What can they discover from their relatives' birth certificates, photo albums, or bibles? For example, are there any common first names? Can the children detect a resemblance between themselves and an aunt, uncle, cousin, or grandparent?

Children of all ages will enjoy *Me and My Family Tree* by Paul Showers, with illustrations by Don Madden. Part of Crowell's "Let's-Read-and-Find-Out Science Books" series, the book clearly explains just what a family tree is and how one inherits certain traits from ancestors.

Another good teacher reference to have on hand is the free brochure, "Suggestions for Beginners in Genealogy," published by the National Genealogy Society, 1921 Sunderland Place N.W., Washington, D.C. 20036. Enclose a stamped, self-addressed envelope with your request.

HOME AND COMMUNITY

Two books for middle- and upper-grade students offer a wealth of activity ideas to extend "roots awareness" in the home and community. Many of the ideas presented can be adapted for primary-grade children, too.

My Backyard History Book by David Weitzman, illustrated by James Robertson, contains exciting innovative approaches for boys and girls no matter who or where they are. Organized around the concept that learning about the past begins best at home, the book explains, among other projects, how to build "A Birthday Time Capsule," construct several types of family trees and time lines, and find history in the cemetery.

Underfoot: An Everyday Guide to Exploring the American Past, also by Weitzman, tells how to find, interpret, and record clues to the past to learn more about our families, our communities, and ourselves. The book explores many ways one can make local history a part of daily life. Among them are how to use tape recorders to interview relatives; how you can learn from, preserve, and copy old photographs; and how to use treasures of data in old newspapers, magazines, and historical journals. Drawings, prints, and black-and-white photographs are also included.

FEELINGS AND ART

Sharing the emotions and thoughts of people who may be very much like some of their own ancestors is another way children can study their pasts. *Tales of the Elders: A Memory Book of Men and Women Who Came to America as Immigrants, 1900–1930,* written and photographed by Carol Ann Bales, includes 12 short interviews with people who migrated to America during the "Great Migration." Readers meet people from the world over who relate how they traveled, what they left behind and why, what they hoped for, what they did, and how they reconstructed their lives in a strange new country.

Studying and making folk art and handicrafts can provide children with more insight into their genealogies. A volume that effectively ties together the subjects of art and culture is *23 Varieties of Ethnic Art and How to Make Each One* by Jean and Cle Kinney. It provides instructions for making such diverse objets d'art as Indonesian batiks, Italian mosaics, and Ukrainian Easter eggs. Although some projects are more difficult than others, readers will find a great deal of information about the people represented and the countries' art heritages. In the Introduction, the authors stress: "By reading about the ethnic group or groups you belong to, you will get a better understanding of your parents and grandparents and begin to see why you think and work as you do. In so doing, you may come to know yourself better." *23 Varieties . . .* might spark plans to stage an ethnic arts festival. Some of the handmade works might be used for gift giving.

FROM ONE BOOK TO MANY

All of these nonfiction titles naturally lead to the wide variety of fiction dealing with ethnic themes. Once children become more aware of themselves and their heritages, they will find learning about others rewarding and challenging.

One powerful, short-titled volume—*Roots*—started us all thinking about our past. There may be no better way to look back than through books.

REFERENCES[2]

Bales, Carol Ann. *Tales of the Elders: A Memory Book of Men and Women Who Came to America as Immigrants, 1900–1930.* Follett, 1977.

[2]See Appendix for publishers' complete addresses.

Canfield, Jack, and Harold C. Wells. *100 Ways to Enhance Self-Concept in the Classroom: A Handbook for Teachers and Parents.* Prentice-Hall, 1976; paperback.

Haley, Alex. *Roots.* Doubleday, 1976; Dell paperback.

Hopkins, Lee Bennett. *Let Them Be Themselves: Language Arts for Children in Elementary Schools.* 2nd Enlarged Edition. Scholastic/Citation Press, 1974; also available in paperback.

Kinney, Jean, and Cle Kinney. *23 Varieties of Ethnic Art and How To Make Each One.* Atheneum, 1976.

Showers, Paul. *Me and My Family Tree.* Crowell, 1978.

Weitzman, David. *My Backyard History Book.* Little, Brown, 1975; also available in paperback.

————. *Underfoot: An Everyday Guide to Exploring the American Past.* Scribner, 1975.

Put a little love in their hearts

Love, it is said, makes the world go round. To help children think about and discuss one of the most important ingredients in our lives, have them circle around while you read them *Around and Around—Love* by Betty Miles. In simple, rhythmic language, the author describes a wide range of expressions of love. Dozens of love-filled black-and-white photographs taken by 28 different photographers enhance this unique volume, making it one for all ages to read, look at, and enjoy.

When you have finished reading the brief text, ask boys and girls to write similes and/or metaphors about love. What would they compare this emotion to? A collection of photographs or those featured in *Around and Around—Love* might be just the thing to spark reactions. Responses can be posted on a "Love Is ..." bulletin board display. Encourage the children to look through newspapers and magazines for photographs or pictures that illustrate what they have written about love and add these to your display.

NOVEL LOVE

Once love has begun to filter through the classroom, don't let it go. Suggest that students design a "Love Scroll" that lists books on this theme. When they find appropriate selections, they can write the book's title, author, and a quote from it on the list. As the scroll unwinds throughout the year, the children will soon realize that love manifests itself in many ways—love for inanimate objects, love for animals, and love among people.

Two picture books for the younger set dealing with love in different phases are *Anna Banana,* written and illustrated by Rosekrans Hoffman, and *I Loved Rose Ann* by Lee Bennett Hopkins. *Anna Banana* tells a romping tale of Charlie and Berthola, a married couple of chimpanzees who loved each other ever since they were in kindergarten. They lead simple, happy lives until their first baby is born. Charlie is positive the new baby is a boy because all first-born babies in *his* family have been of the male gender. When the baby arrives, Charlie names him James Charles, not knowing it is a girl. Berthola doesn't have the heart to tell him that their he is really a she! When the big day approaches for James Charles to be intro- duced to all the relatives, Charlie finds out about his "son's" identity in a surprising and tender conclusion. Hoffman's line drawings add greatly to this truly unusual tale.

I Loved Rose Ann presents a two-part story about the thwarted romance between two youngsters, Harry Hooper and Rose Ann. Harry Hooper loves Rose Ann but he just can't understand why she doesn't return the feeling. Readers find out via Rose Ann's side of the story that she really does like Harry Hooper and that the entire escapade is all a misunderstanding. Pen-and-ink sketches are by Ingred Fetz.

Three classics in children's literature warmly illustrate other variations. *The Velveteen Rabbit* by Margery Williams, first published in 1926, is one of the earliest stories to personify toys. Any girl or boy who loves or has loved a stuffed animal will relate to the tale of a plush bunny who comes to life because of love. This heartwarming story, illustrated by William Nichol- son, is also available as a sound filmstrip set from Miller-Brody Productions, Inc., with the noted Eva Le Gallienne doing the narration.

Woven through *Charlotte's Web* by E. B. White is even more love. The fantasy about the spider, Charlotte A. Cavatica, who befriends a pig, spins and plaits the themes of life, friendship, and fondness. Many children will have an easy time selecting passages from this heralded book, illustrated by Garth Wil- liams.

In the last chapter of *A Wrinkle in Time,* the 1963 Newbery Award winning-book by Madeleine L'Engle, Charles Wallace is saved from the strange IT of Camazotz by love. That's the one thing Charlie's sister, Meg Murray, has that IT does not. To her brother, who is in a faraway trance, she calls, "Come back to me, Charles Wallace, come away from IT, come back, come home. I love you, Charles. Oh, Charles Wallace, I love you." The power of love eventually wins out, even over IT!

To highlight these and other renowned books on love, students can construct bookstore-like displays. Brightly drawn pictures, toys, or handmade models based on the books' characters and settings will draw even reluctant readers to see what is inside.

POETRY PEG

A Poetry Hunt for love themes is a lively technique to keep good feelings flowing in the classroom. Ask the children to seek examples in original volumes of poetry and in anthologies to share at planned poetry reading sessions. Individual students or small groups can act out or mime a poem, sing it, set a recitation to music, or tape record it with background sound effects.

Plant a PoeTree that will blossom with verses. Branches can be attached to a wall, hung from the ceiling like a mobile, or placed in a pail or flowerpot filled with sand, earth, or styrofoam. Spray paint can change the color of the branches from time to time. As children select and illustrate favorite poems, they can be attached to the branches for others to read. In New Jersey, a fourth-grade teacher has each child create mini-Poe-Trees as gifts for parents. Each child decorates a cardboard milk carton, fills it with earth, and then places a small twig firmly inside. At the top of the branch some children place pictures of themselves or of the person who is going to receive the gift. The mini-PoeTrees are unique, unusual, inexpensive, and very effective presents to make, give, and receive.

Love poems for older boys and girls can be found in the section, "Soullove" in *On Our Way: Poems of Pride and Love,* selected by Lee Bennett Hopkins. Dramatic brown-tone photographs by David Parks illustrate four poems by Dudley Randall, Mari Evans, Quandra Prettyman, and Raymond Richard Patterson.

One Little Room, an Everywhere: Poems of Love, edited by Myra Cohn Livingston, is divided into three parts—"Hopes," "Joys," and "Sorrows." The anthology contains poetry from Biblical times to the present and from many nations—China, Russia, Spain, Chile, England, and the United States. The universality of the selections makes this book a good tie-in for social studies in the upper grades.

Put a little love in their hearts—with children's books. We can all—always—use some!

REFERENCES[1]

Hoffman, Rosekrans. *Anna Banana.* Knopf, 1975.

Hopkins, Lee Bennett. *I Loved Rose Ann.* Knopf, 1976; Xerox paperback.

———. *On Our Way: Poems of Pride and Love.* Knopf, 1974.

L'Engle, Madeleine. *A Wrinkle in Time.* Farrar, Straus, 1962; Dell paperback.

Livingston, Myra Cohn. *One Little Room, an Everywhere: Poems of Love.* Atheneum, 1975.

Miles, Betty. *Around and Around—Love.* Knopf, 1975; also available in paperback.

White, E. B. *Charlotte's Web.* Harper & Row, 1952; also available in paperback.

Williams, Margery. *The Velveteen Rabbit.* Doubleday, 1926; Avon paperback.

[1]See Appendix for publishers' complete addresses.

PART III

Children and Culture

The eyes of children are upon it:
Books and television

Facts about children's television viewing habits are overwhelming: the average child watches approximately 4000 hours of television before he or she even enters the first grade and 15,000 hours before high school graduation. The question is no longer, "What can we do *about* it?" but "What can we do *with* it?"

To help children become more aware of the time they spend in front of the television set, have them set up a daily viewing log for a week or two, including weekends. Students can record the programs they watch and the number of hours of viewing time. A tally of the total may surprise them, especially when compared to the amount of time they spend sleeping, eating, and going to school.

Next, discuss the various types of programs noted in the logs. This will provide clues as to the children's interests and a starting point for mixing good reading with television viewing.

Teachers, librarians, publishers, and booksellers with whom I have worked and interviewed note that demands for titles coinciding with book-based television programs are especially high. For example, sales of Laura Ingalls Wilder's books, the basis for the television series, *Little House on the Prairie* (NBC), have soared—more than tripled—since the first episode appeared several years ago. To highlight titles that tie in with television series and specials, ask student volunteers to organize a "What's on TV?" committee. Their function will be to scan *TV Guide,* local newspapers, and magazines to alert class-mates to better television fare. Encourage the committee to work with the school librarian to locate titles that are adapted from programs or that complement specific shows.

In one fourth-grade classroom, the children viewed an epi-sode of *Wild Kingdom* (NBC), that featured alligators. Before-hand, the committee distributed a duplicated reminder that each child took home, and set up a display of related books. Two of the books—*The Moon of the Alligators* by Jean Craighead George, illustrated by Adriana Zanazanian, and *The Alligator Book: 60 Questions and Answers* by William Bentley—were never more desired or read. The same technique can be used for camels, koalas, or kangaroos!

The *ABC-TV After-School Specials* are worth watching for. Programs, adapted from children's books, include "Sara's Sum-mer of the Swans" from Betsy Byars Newbery Award-winning novel, *The Summer of the Swans:* "The Pinballs," also based on the book by Byars; and "The Street of the Flower Boxes," from Peggy Mann's book of the same title. Since reruns are common, seek out titles well before their air dates for students to read. After they have seen the programs, hold a discussion on the similarities and differences between the televised and printed versions. Discussion questions such as the following should start the children on their way to analyzing the differences:

• Were the characters portrayed as you visualized them when you read the book?
• Were the characters as appealing in the media presenta-tion?
• Were any characters added? Eliminated? Was this neces-sary?
• What events did the media presentation highlight from the book's plot?
• Were there any important episodes left out? Anything added? Did it make it better or worse?
• Would you rather read an author's words about something or see a visual account?
• If you were the author of the book, what things would you have liked about the media presentation? What would you have disliked?
• Did the musical background and/or other special effects help recreate the mood of the book? How?

• If you hadn't read the book before, would you want to read it after seeing it televised?

Popular television shows have also spawned several books for children. "The House Without a Christmas Tree," first introduced as an award-winning CBS special, is available in book form by Gail Rock, illustrated by Charles G. Gehm. Three additional titles by Rock also went from the screen into print, creating a classic heroine in Addie Mills: *A Dream for Addie* (televised as "The Easter Promise"), *The Thanksgiving Treasure* (both illustrated by Gehm), and *Addie and the King of Hearts,* illustrated by Charles McVicker. These warm, family stories, set in the 1940s in a small Nebraska town, depict a girl growing up—her feelings, problems, and reactions to varied life situations.

Maurice Sendak's *Really Rosie Starring the Nutshell Kids* stemmed from a CBS special. An attractive, oversized paperback edition contains the scenario, plus music and lyrics by Carole King. Also available is a recording of the songs and the program itself in a variety of audiovisual media from Weston Woods. The total package provides everything you'll need to spark classroom or assembly productions.

Many television viewers like to discuss the pros and cons of their favorite or least favorite programs. Children are no exception. A debate forum is one way to air viewpoints. Or, if your students have a pen pal letter exchange with youngsters in another town or state, encourage them to trade opinions. A foreign pen pal can offer fascinating insights on television programming in his or her country, too.

WHAT'S THE WEATHER LIKE?

A combination of television and books can be an effective introduction or supplement to classroom studies. For example, before students get involved in the highs and lows of meteorology, ask them to tune in to a daily television weather report. They may find that the barrage of words, terms, and symbols is so overwhelming that they won't know what the weather will be like tomorrow! Three books can help define the complicated terminology and enhance science units.

What children have always wanted to know about weather and are not afraid to ask is in *Questions and Answers About Weather* by M. Jean Craig. Delightful colorful illustrations by

Judy Craig accompany the explanations to such queries as "Do clouds freeze in cold weather?" and "What is a rainbow?"

Experiments for children to perform and directions for things to make, like an anemometer and a rain gauge, are included in *Weather All Around* by Tillie S. Pine and Joseph Levine, illustrated by Bernice Myers. *Weather or Not* by Wallene T. Dockery, illustrated by Steve Laughbaum, is an informative account of weather encased in fiction form.

BEHIND-THE-SCREEN JOBS

Just reading the list of credits that rolls by at a program's end will give children some idea of the many different jobs in broadcasting. A tour of a local station is one way to see television personnel in action. But there's one kind of specialist that the children may have already met in their own living rooms —the TV repairer. To help children see the skills involved in this job, invite a repairer to the classroom and scout around for an old discarded portable TV set. Ask the technician to take it apart, explaining in simple terms what the major parts are and how they bring moving, talking pictures to the screen.

Two good titles to have on hand before, during, and after such an event are *What Makes TV Work?* by Scott Corbett, illustrated by Len Darwin, and *See Inside a TV Studio* by George Beal, illustrated in full color by John Berry and John Marshall. Corbett's book details the sequence of steps necessary to transmit a television picture from the studio to the home receiver; Beal's volume tells how the camera and different kinds of recording devices work, how special effects are produced, and how television is transmitted via satellite. Also included are historical background and job descriptions of all personnel involved in this complex and fascinating industry.

Of course, all of television broadcasting is the result of a team effort, especially news reporting. For a detailed look at careers in this field, channel students' attention to *Finding Out About Jobs: TV Reporting*, written and illustrated by Jeanne and Robert Bendick. The authors describe numerous job roles, along with activities that challenge girls and boys to try things on their own.

The Incredible Television Machine by Lee Polk and Eda Le Shan gives readers information as to how television shows are put together, and discusses the influence television has on everyday life and how viewers' opinions can change and affect television programming. The book, illustrated in black-and-white line drawings by Roy Doty, includes a listing of books for further reading and an index.

Older readers will enjoy *Women in Television* by Anita Klever, which depicts the limitations and drawbacks as well as the excitement of jobs in the industry. A representative sampling of main job areas are discussed, including program director, producer, and anchorperson.

Another interesting title to share with older students is *Who Puts the News on TV?* by Barbara Steinberg, one of the titles in the "Adventures in the World of Work" paperback series published by Random House. This volume, illustrated with photographs, features first-person accounts with workers who discuss the pros and cons of their job roles, day-to-day routines, the rewards and challenges, and the training and education required.

FOR THE PROFESSIONAL SHELF

Two nonprofit organizations are well worth knowing about—Action for Children's Television (ACT), 46 Austin Street, Newtonville, Massachusetts 02160; and Agency for Instructional Television (AIT), Box A, Bloomington, Indiana 47401. A postcard will place you on their mailing lists to receive news and information.

Aims of ACT are:

1. To encourage the development and enforcement of appropriate guidelines relating to children and the media;
2. To pressure and persuade broadcasters and advertisers to provide programming of the highest possible quality designed for children of different ages;
3. To encourage research, experimentation, and evaluation in the field of children's television.

AIT, an American–Canadian organization, was established in 1973 to strengthen education through television and other technologies. The organization develops joint program projects involving state and provincial agencies, and acquires and distributes a wide variety of television and related printed materials for use as major learning resources. It makes many of the television materials available in audiovisual formats. AIT's predecessor organization, National Instructional Television, was founded in 1962. This group offers a free quarterly publication, "Newsletter," containing information on its educational programs (such as *Inside/Out, Bread and Butterflies,* and *Zebra Wings*), listings of upcoming events and workshops, and new programs being produced.

Two excellent adult books to share with parents are Marie Winn's *The Plug-In Drug: Television, Children and the Family,* and Evelyn Kaye's *The Family Guide to Children's Television: What to Watch, What to Miss, What to Change and How to Do It.* Winn's book, based on interviews with hundreds of families, teachers, and child specialists, presents a frightening picture of a society dominated by television; of children with poor verbal skills, an inability to concentrate, and a disinclination to read; and of parents who are "hooked" on using television as a sedative for their preschool children. Kaye's volume, prepared under the guidance of ACT with the cooperation of the American Academy of Pediatrics, is an informative guide to help parents solve the dilemmas about television. An excellent, 19-page "Resource Directory" is appended.

A current source to aid you in the classroom is "TV Talk" by Rosemary Lee Potter, a monthly feature column that appears in *Teacher* magazine.

SIGN-OFF

In an article, "How TV Helps Johnny Read" by Max Gunther,[1] Dr. Michael McAndrew, a reading expert in the Philadelphia school system, stated: "For much too long TV and the world of literary education have been barking and snapping at each other ... they can work together in peace ... each can profit enormously from having the other around. It's a fantastic marriage between two old enemies."

As educators, all of us must work together to make "the fantastic marriage" go smoothly!

REFERENCES[2]

Beal, George. *See Inside a TV Studio.* Watts, 1978.
Bendick, Jeanne, and Robert Bendick. *Finding Out About Jobs: TV Reporting.* Parents' Magazine Press, 1976.

[1] *TV Guide,* September 4, 1976, page 10.
[2] See Appendix for publishers' complete addresses.

Bentley, William. *The Alligator Book: 60 Questions and Answers.* Walker, 1977.

Byars, Betsy. *The Pinballs.* Harper & Row, 1977; also available in paperback.

———. *The Summer of the Swans.* Viking, 1970; Avon paperback.

Craig, M. Jean. *Questions and Answers About the Weather.* Four Winds, 1973.

Corbett, Scott. *What Makes TV Work?* Little, Brown, 1965.

Dockery, Wallene T. *Weather or Not.* Abingdon, 1976.

George, Jean Craighead. *The Moon of the Alligators.* Crowell, 1969.

Kaye, Evelyn. *The Family Guide to Children's Television: What to Watch, What to Miss, What to Change and How to Do it.* Pantheon, 1974; also available in paperback.

Klever, Anita. *Women in TV.* Westminster, 1976.

Mann, Peggy. *The Street of the Flower Boxes.* Coward McCann, 1966; Archway paperback.

Pine, Tillie S., and Joseph Levine. *Weather All Around.* McGraw-Hill, 1966.

Polk, Lee, and Eda Le Shan. *The Incredible Television Machine.* Macmillan, 1977.

Rock, Gail. *Addie and the King of Hearts.* Knopf, 1975; Bantam paperback.

———. *A Dream for Addie.* Knopf, 1975; Bantam paperback.

———. *The House Without A Christmas Tree.* Knopf, 1974; Bantam paperback.

———. *The Thanksgiving Treasure.* Knopf, 1974; Bantam paperback.

Sendak, Maurice. *Really Rosie Starring the Nutshell Kids.* Harper & Row paperback, 1975.

Steinberg, Barbara. *Who Puts the News on TV?* Random House paperback, 1976.

Wilder, Laura Ingalls. *The Little House* series, illustrated by Garth Williams. Harper & Row, 1953; available in paperback.

Winn, Marie. *The Plug-In Drug: Television, Children and the Family.* Viking, 1977; Bantam paperback.

The fine arts:
Worlds for seeing, moving, and growing

Grandma Moses, van Gogh, and Nureyev once sat behind desks in classrooms somewhere. By opening up the world of art to children, we can begin to nurture awareness and—who knows?—future artists. A number of exciting children's books that focus on painting, sculpture, and dance offer rich opportunities for discovery and exploration, allowing each child to see his or her own style, taste, and creative forces.

BASIC TECHNIQUES

To introduce children to the fundamentals of the visual arts and the insights art can provide, offer them the beautifully designed and illustrated 1970 Newbery Honor book, *The Many Ways of Seeing: An Introduction to the Pleasures of Art* by Janet Gaylord Moore. In her introduction the author states: "The ways in which you look at the world of nature and the world of art can help you understand yourself and what kind of person you choose to become. Your own experiences of life can, in turn, broaden and deepen your understanding of this language of arts." Illustrated with 80 black-and-white and 32 full-color reproductions of great paintings, student photographs, and drawings, the volume points out that there are, indeed, *many* ways of seeing.

Moore lucidly explains form, line, color, and texture, and

encourages readers to try their own techniques. Of particular interest is the chapter, "Interlude: A Collage of Pictures and Quotations," which can spark activity ideas for students of all ages. For example, children can compare and contrast the imagery, feelings, and thoughts expressed in the black-and-white print, "The Old Guitarist" by Picasso with five stanzas from the poem, "The Man with the Blue Guitar" by Wallace Stevens. To supplement this activity, students can collect photographs, reproductions, and/or original drawings. They can add literary quotations to their finds by checking the index of *Bartlett's Familiar Quotations* by John Bartlett to locate an appropriate match, or they can look through favorite books with themes similar to the pictorials.

You and your students can share more descriptive pictures and words with *Pieter Brueghel's The Fair* by Ruth F. Craft. This picture book interprets in lilting verse some of the many details in the painting *The Village Fair.* A full-color reproduction of the painting and close-up views appear with appropriate text. This kind of book not only shows children the importance of looking at a picture carefully and thoughtfully but also promotes descriptive and analytical writing about what they see.

MASTERS OF EXPRESSION

Every artist has a unique style of expression. To help children detect individual characteristics and identify the work of particular artists, try "Art for Children Series" by Adeline Peter and Ernest Raboff. Currently there are 15 volumes which concentrate on such masters as da Vinci, Velázquez, Picasso, van Gogh, and Renoir. Each book explains the characteristic techniques, analyzes 15 full-color reproductions of paintings, drawings, and sculpture, and offers a brief biographical sketch of and quotes by each artist. For a complete list of titles and order information, write to the publisher to request a brochure.

As the children's familiarity with this subject grows, you can involve the entire class or appoint a committee to set out on an art and artist hunt. Have them find and bring to class prints and mount them to begin a class art file. Often, local art-supply stores and museum shops offer many inexpensive reproductions that are ideal for this purpose. A good source for full-color reproductions or photographs at nominal cost is Giant Photos,

Inc. Send for a brochure to find out what meets your specific grade or interest level needs. Whenever the students make additions to the file, encourage them to think about and discuss the pictures. For example, you might pose these questions: How does he or she draw attention to an important part of the composition? What does the work reveal about the dress, manners, and customs of the particular subject, place, or time depicted?

If possible, display examples of similar paintings from the file on one theme, such as landscapes, children, flowers, or animals, or have students compare several paintings by the same artist. This exercise can help them become better acquainted with various techniques and with the identification of a particular artist's work.

For the classroom or school library reference shelf, you may want to investigate "The World of Art" series published by Oxford University Press. Although these 50 handsome paperbacks are geared to adult audiences, they can serve as useful reference tools for middle and upper graders. The books are organized in three categories: "Surveys," such as *African Art* by Frank Willett; "Periods and Movements," such as *Greek Art* by John Boardman; "Artists," such as *Bruegel* by Walter S. Gibson.

THREE DIMENSIONS

Studying three-dimensional line, form, color, and texture via sculpture can be the basis for fascinating trips to local parks, historical sites, museums, and even cemeteries. After students examine sculptural works in stone, metal, wood, or other materials, ask them to research the answers to the following questions: Who did the sculpture? Why? What does it represent?

One introductory volume written by an experienced museum educator that can aid in finding answers to the above questions is *Looking at Sculpture* by Roberta M. Paine. This volume covers a wide range of works, from ancient to modern, and is illustrated with black-and-white photographs. An index is appended.

CREATIVE MOVEMENT

Dance is an art form that most children relish and want to imitate at the sound of the first note. Several titles convey so much of the joy and enchantment of this medium that you may see a conga line of eager readers awaiting their turn for them.

Even the youngest will get up on his or her toes after reading or listening to *Sometimes I Dance Mountains* by Byrd Baylor. Herein a young dancer invites readers to dance like mountains, whirlwinds, bubbles, and bugs! The well-designed text features black-and-white photographs by Bill Sears and magical mystical line drawings by Ken Longtemps. With the aid of the physical education instructor, dance movements can be introduced in gym classes via a title such as this.

During the month of December, chances are that some nearby dance company will be presenting a version of *The Nutcracker.* If you can arrange a class trip to this production, it will be well worth the effort. But if such an excursion isn't possible, children can become familiar with the basic story line by reading *The Nutcracker,* retold by Toshiko Yamanushi (English version by Alvin Tresselt). This picture book treatment based on E. T. A. Hoffmann's tale, which was the inspiration for Tchaikovsky's classic *Nutcracker Suite,* has full-color illustrations by Seiichi Horiuchi. Girls and boys of all ages will also enjoy Martha Swope's *The Nutcracker: The Story of the New York City Ballet's Production Told in Pictures.* The simple text, together with black-and-white photographs, describe the action of this world-famous ballet production.

There's more to dance than beautiful costumes and scenery, of course. As two books for mature readers aptly point out, hard work and effort come first. *A Very Young Dancer* written and photographed by Jill Krementz, relates a child's experiences as she tries out and lands a leading role in the New York City Ballet's *Nutcracker. A Young Person's Guide to Ballet* by Noel Streatfield follows two more young ballet students over a 3-year period. Basic ballet steps, the history of the dance, discussions of several ballet films, and stories and personalities of past and present balletomanes are interwoven. Line drawings and black-and-white photographs are by Georgette Bordier.

In *A Midsummer Night's Dream,* Martha Swope gives readers a treat from curtain time to curtain call. Her photography captures the magic of a ballet performance in which fairies and humans are turned topsy-turvy by the antics of the mischievous Puck. Captions by Nancy Lassalle tell the story. Also included are quotations from the play by William Shakespeare and an introduction by Lincoln Kirstein. Another volume sure to be well-read and well-loved is the lavish and popular collection of six ballet stories, *The Royal Book of Ballet* by Shirley Goulden, illustrated by Maraja.

An excellent adult reference book to refer to is *The Encyclopedia of Dance and Ballet,* edited by Mary Clarke and David Vaughan, containing over 2000 entries covering ballet and contemporary dance, defined as "any form of dance raised to a theatrical level." The text is arranged alphabetically, is fully cross-referenced and includes entries written by an expert in his or her field. The book is illustrated with 24 full-color plates and over 200 black-and-white photographs. A glossary of technical terms is appended.

The quotation from the French novelist Marcel Proust, perhaps best sums up the benefits of studying the fine arts: "Thanks to art, instead of seeing a single world, our own, we see it multiply until we have before us as many worlds as there are original artists. . . ."

With children and the arts, the view into these worlds are indeed limitless.

REFERENCES[1]

Bartlett, John. *Bartlett's Familiar Quotations.* Little, Brown, 1968.

Baylor, Byrd. *Sometimes I Dance Mountains.* Scribner, 1973.

Clarke, Mary, and David Vaughan, eds. *The Encyclopedia of Dance and Ballet.* Putnam, 1977.

Craft, Ruth F. *Pieter Brueghel's The Fair.* Lippincott, 1975.

Goulden, Shirley. *The Royal Book of Ballet,* illustrated by Maraja. Follett, 1964.

Krementz, Jill. *A Very Young Dancer.* Knopf. 1976.

Moore, Janet Gaylord. *The Many Ways of Seeing: An Introduction to the Pleasures of Art.* Collins+World, 1969.

Paine, Roberta M. *Looking at Sculpture.* Lothrop, 1968.

Peter, Adeline, and Ernest Raboff. *Art for Children* series. Doubleday, 15 vols.

Streatfield, Noel. *A Young Person's Guide to Ballet.* Warne, 1975.

Swope, Martha. *The Nutcracker: The Story of the New York City Ballet's Production Told in Pictures.* Dodd, Mead, 1975.

———. *A Midsummer Night's Dream.* Dodd, Mead, 1977.

World of Art series. Oxford University Press, 50 vols.

Yamanushi, Toshiko. *The Nutcracker.* English edition by Alvin Tresselt, illustrated by Seiichi Horiuchi. Parents' Magazine Press, 1974.

[1]See Appendix for publishers' complete addresses.

Globe trotting with poetry

Poetry reflects people, their lifestyles, experiences, dreams, feelings, and ideas. It is a universal form of creative communication, yet each poem has a unique "personality." By learning what poets from all over the world have to say, children can better understand how all people are alike and yet different.

A world-poetry hunt is a good way to start globe-trotting. Post maps of the United States and the world on a bulletin board. Underneath it, set up a table display of books featuring the poetry of both American and foreign poets. As children find, read, and share selections, they can mark off places on the maps where the verses originated.

POEMS FROM HOME

America is rich in a wide number of natural resources, not the least of which is poetry for children. To emphasize the regional, cultural, and social influences that poetry can reveal, have the students discuss verses they especially enjoy and then ask each child to research the part of the country that his or her favorite poet comes from. Sometimes this information is readily found on book jackets. As the children's repertoires grow, they will begin to see that poets come from all walks of life and environs. Some of the leading American poets they will want to encounter are: David McCord from Massachusetts; Nikki

Giovanni, New York; Lucille Clifton, Maryland; Gwendolyn Brooks, Illinois; Aileen Fisher, Colorado; and Myra Cohn Livingston, California.

Solicit the children's opinions on the poems they have read. Do they feel the lines provide a good picture of where the poet lives or how she or he thinks or feels? Why? Ask them if they can spot similarities or differences among such collections as *Bronzeville Boys and Girls* by Gwendolyn Brooks, illustrated by Ronni Solbert; Nikki Giovanni's *Ego-Tripping and Other Poems for Young People,* illustrated by George Ford, and *Spin A Soft Black Song: Poems for Children,* illustrated by Charles Bible; *The Malibu and Other Poems* by Myra Cohn Livingston, illustrated by James Spanfeller; and *Feathered Ones and Furry* by Aileen Fisher, illustrated by Eric Carle.

WORLD PIPERS

Exciting volumes of poetry that can help children gain new insights about world neighbors and their cultures have been published in recent years. Although several are in picture-book format, girls and boys of all ages will enjoy them because of their varied and unique presentations. For example, some of the books include foreign translations of poems. Two bountiful anthologies of this kind are *Have You Seen a Comet?: Children's Art and Writing from Around the World,* edited by Anne Pellowski, Helen R. Sattley, and Joyce C. Arkhurst; and *A Tune Beyond Us: A Collection of Poems,* edited by Myra Cohn Livingston, illustrated by James Spanfeller. The first contains poems, letters, anecdotes, stories, essays, and illustrations by children and teenagers from the United States and major foreign countries, plus Liberia, Czechoslovakia, Turkey, Costa Rica, Malaysia, and Poland. In *A Tune Beyond Us,* Livingston, a well-loved poet herself, has gathered a rich collection to introduce students to world poetry. Here children can see verses printed in Latin, Chinese, Spanish, Italian German, French, and Russian, all accompanied by translations.

Another attractive combination of language and verse is *Chinese Mother Goose Rhymes,* selected and edited by Robert Wyndham. Designed to be read vertically, the Chinese calligraphy ornaments the margins of each page. Forty traditional rhymes, riddles, lullabies, and games that have amused Chinese children for generations are included. Full-color illustrations are by the Caldecott Honor Book winner, Ed Young.

THE MUSIC OF WORDS

A poem, like a song, is meant to be heard. Consider arranging a classroom visit by people who can read other languages, so that the children can enjoy the "music" of the words. With older students, this can lead to a discussion of translating—why and how it is done, who does it, and what happens to the original meaning of the words and poetic forms.

For example, in haiku, a Japanese unrhymed poetic form that many children are familiar with, each poem is composed of seventeen syllables. However, due to the language differences, English translations contain fewer syllables. In any case, haiku's simplicity will motivate children to create their own brief thoughts about nature and/or the seasons. You will find some excellent examples of traditional haiku verse in *Cricket Songs: Japanese Haiku* and *More Cricket Songs: Japanese Haiku,* both translated by Harry Behn. A delightful bonus is the accompanying black-and-white prints chosen from the works of Sesshu, a Japanese master artist, and others. In *A Few Flies and I: Haiku by Issa,* selected by Jean Merrill and Ronni Solbert and illustrated by Ronni Solbert, a brief 7-page "Introduction to Issa" not only gives children an idea of what haiku is really written about but also presents a glimpse of a poor, solitary man who created almost 1000 verses on such creatures as snails, toads, frogs, fireflies, and fleas!

Two other popular collections of haiku are *In a Spring Garden,* with poems selected by Richard Lewis (also available as a 16mm film or filmstrip/book/record combination from Weston Woods), accompanied by full-color collage illustrations by Caldecott Award winner Ezra Jack Keats; and *Don't Tell the Scarecrow and Other Japanese Poems* by Issa, Yayu, Kikaku, and other Japanese poets, illustrated by Tālavaldis Stubis.

Asia has also given us sijo, Korean narrative poetry. Introduce students to this kind of verse with *Sunset in a Spider Web: Sijo Poetry of Ancient Korea,* selected by Virginia Olsen Baron and illustrated by Minja Park Kim. In her "Introduction," Baron explains that sijo poems were written to be sung while the rhythm was beaten on a drum to lute accompaniment. With coffee-can drums, a recorder, and a little practice, children can do likewise to set these or their own original sijo creations to made-up rhythms.

CHILDREN'S VOICES

Collections of poetry written by children can have special appeal. They draw young readers closer to faraway peers and encourage similar creativity. One of the finest volumes of this kind to appear is *Miracles: Poems by Children of the English-Speaking World,* collected by Richard Lewis. Its subtle message is that no matter where children live and write, whether it is in the United States, Kenya, Uganda, or Australia, they all have one thing in common—they are all children. Universal themes about playing, people, feelings, and the seasons are expressed by writers between the ages of 5 and 13.

Another sure to be well-thumbed volume from a part of the world we know little about is *The Moon is Like a Silver Sickle: A Celebration of Poetry by Russian Children,* collected and translated by Miriam Morton. The 92 poems are written in a variety of forms by children between the ages of 4 and 14 and are divided into six themes. Brown-tone illustrations are by Eros Keith.

Poems by Jewish and Arab children who have witnessed war, slept in shelters and, unfortunately, known too much about death are featured in *My Shalom, My Peace* by Jacob Zim *et al.* The young writers look beyond their world of hatred and destruction to a single fragile concept that they have never experienced—peace. Several selections are printed in both the original language and the English translation. Over 36 color and line drawings and 26 halftones contribute to a book that is a testimony to the entire world.

POETRY PARTING IDEAS

Perhaps groups of children would like to design and make minianthologies as gifts to next year's incoming class, the school library, or parents. One group might plan a Poetry Atlas featuring poems from continent to continent and illustrate them with original drawings and appropriate sections cut from world maps.

Large, illustrated bookmarks for children, featuring the work of four contemporary poets who use joy as their theme, are truly joyous gifts to keep poetry blossoming. The selections include free verse by Nikki Giovanni; a concrete, or shaped poem by Robert Froman; a limerick by X. J. Kennedy; and a cinquain by Eve Merriam. The backs of each bookmark are blank, perfect for children to record poetry volumes they love or want to seek out on library shelves, or for creating their own verse. The bookmarks are available in packages of 100 from the Children's Book Council.

For serious-minded upper-grade poetry enthusiasts who want to spend time refining their own writing, suggest *The Poet's Eye: An Introduction to Poetry for Young People* by Arthur Alexander, illustrated by Colleen Browning. The chapter "Kinds of Poetry" introduces a range of forms from couplets and light and humorous verses to sonnets. A glossary of poetic terms and an index are appended.

Like the promise proclaimed by an old Navy recruiting slogan, poetry offers children many not-to-be-missed experiences, sights, sounds, ideas, and feelings. Join up and see the world!

REFERENCES[1]

Alexander, Arthur. *The Poet's Eye: An Introduction to Poetry for Young People.* Prentice-Hall, 1967.

Baron, Virginia Olsen, ed. *Sunset in a Spider Web: Sijo Poetry of Ancient Korea.* Holt, Rinehart and Winston, 1974.

Behn, Harry, trans. *Cricket Songs: Japanese Haiku.* Harcourt, 1964.

———, trans. *More Cricket Songs: Japanese Haiku.* Harcourt, 1971.

Brooks, Gwendolyn. *Bronzeville Boys and Girls.* Harper & Row, 1956.

Fisher, Aileen. *Feathered Ones and Furry.* Crowell, 1971.

Giovanni, Nikki. *Ego-Tripping and Other Poems for Young People.* Lawrence Hill, 1973.

———. *Spin A Soft Black Song: Poems for Children.* Hill and Wang, 1971.

Issa. *A Few Flies and I: Haiku by Issa,* edited by Jean Merrill and Ronni Solbert. Pantheon, 1969.

Issa et al. *Don't Tell the Scarecrow and Other Japanese Poems.* Four Winds, 1979; Scholastic paperback.

Lewis, Richard, ed. *In A Spring Garden.* Dial, 1965; also available in paperback.

[1]See Appendix for publishers' complete addresses.

————, ed. *Miracles: Poems by Children of the English-Speaking World.* Simon & Schuster, 1966; Bantam paperback.

Livingston, Myra Cohn, ed. *A Tune Beyond Us: A Collection of Poems.* Harcourt, 1968.

————. *The Malibu and Other Poems.* Atheneum, 1972.

Morton, Miriam, comp. and trans. *The Moon is Like a Silver Sickle: A Celebration of Poetry by Russian Children.* Simon & Schuster, 1972.

Pellowski, Anne, Helen R. Sattley, and Joyce C. Arkhurst, eds. *Have You Seen a Comet?: Children's Art and Writing from Around the World.* John Day, 1971.

Wyndham, Robert. *Chinese Mother Goose Rhymes.* Collins+World, 1968.

Zim, Jacob et al. *My Shalom, My Peace.* McGraw-Hill, 1975.

13

Music:
Joyful noises and other agreeable sounds

Music and books can well bring children closer together. When children are singing, playing instruments, or experimenting with musical forms, classrooms can truly ring!

Songfests always sound better when accompanied by instruments, whether they are electric guitars or drums made from old coffee cans. If you don't have a class band, you might like to organize one. Begin with a group of volunteers and then rotate positions among other children who wish to perform. This will give students who play specific instruments a chance to display talents and perhaps introduce nonplayers to a new interest.

MAKE YOUR OWN KIND OF MUSIC

Girls and boys of all ages enjoy making their own kind of music. While some students are tuning up for the band, others can begin constructing instruments for subsequent jam sessions. Two titles offer a score of how-tos. *Music and Instruments for Children to Make* and *Rhythms, Music and Instruments to Make*, both by John Hawkinson and Martha Faulhaber, contain a wide variety of activities and easy-to-follow instructions on putting together and using handmade instruments, such as panpipes, drums, and a box harp.

With their hands full of newly made instruments, classroom musicians will be well-equipped for an exploration of basic musical ideas. *Music: Invent Your Own* by Martha Faulhaber and Janet Underhill clearly explains the terms *rhythm*, *timbre*, *melody*, and *dynamics*, and encourages children to express feelings and experiences through sound.

SHOW A FILM, SING A SONG

As music begins to fill the classroom air, stock a shelf with books that truly sing. For further motivation, fill the movie screen with melodious sounds, too. *American Songfest* is a delightful film produced by Weston Woods, Inc., hosted by the Caldecott Award winner, Robert McCloskey, who appears barefoot in a bathtub. He takes viewers on visits to the homes and studios of four creative people who have devised picture books based on songs from American folklore and history. We meet illustrator Steven Kellogg and see portions of the film version of his book, *Yankee Doodle*, with lyrics by Edward Bangs; illustrator Robert Quackenbush and a film version of *She'll Be Comin' 'Round the Mountain*, presented in the format of an old-fashioned lantern show; singer Pete Seeger and an animation of *The Foolish Frog*, written with Charles Seeger and illustrated by Miloslav Jager; and Caldecott Award winner Peter Spier with portions of the film version of *The Star-Spangled Banner*. As an introduction or finale to *American Songfest*, have copies of the books readily available. As boys and girls explore each volume, all with four-color illustrations plus music and lyrics, you may be treated to impromptu "hum-alongs."

After children "meet" such an illustrator as Quackenbush, it will be an easy task to lead them to other titles in his Americana series of picture songbooks. Among them are: *Clementine, Go Tell Aunt Rhody, The Man on the Flying Trapeze, Old MacDonald Had a Farm, Skip to My Lou, There'll Be a Hot Time in the Old Town Tonight,* and the double treat in one book of *Pop! Goes the Weasel* and *Yankee Doodle.* Each book contains historical facts about the song's origin and illustrations, which are based on authentic prints and photographs of the period— good supplements for American history lessons. Blended in are Quackenbush's own brand of humor and some surprises. For example, in *There'll Be a Hot Time . . .* he gives advice on " . . . Your Own Survival Plan and How to Escape from a Burning

Building." In *Pop! Goes the Weasel . . .* , he cites "Eighteen Places to Visit on Your 1776 Tour of Manhattan Island," along with a map of Lower Manhattan; and in *Clementine* he includes instructions on how to pan for gold!

SELECTIONS AND COLLECTIONS

Songbook collections can be valuable timesavers when you are looking for musical sources. Leafing through the pages will inspire children to compile their own anthologies of favorites, create their own tunes, or write additional lyrics or paradies for popular songs.

Children learning to play recorders, or those who already can, can tootle or sing 13 easy rounds about animals in *Sweetly Sings the Donkey: Animal Rounds for Children to Sing or Play on Recorders.* The old and new tunes selected by John Langstaff come from Belgium, England, Scotland, and Czechoslovakia. Stylistic medieval drawings by Nancy Winslow Parker will appeal to the eyes as much as the songs do to the ears.

Rising from a rich cultural tradition, 24 black American spirituals get distinguished treatment in *Walk Together Children: Black American Spirituals,* selected and illustrated with dynamic black-and-white woodcuts by Ashley Bryan. Words and music include universal favorites such as "Swing Low, Sweet Chariot, "Free at Last," and "Nobody Knows the Trouble I See."

Poetry and music have always gone hand in hand. In *The Moon on the One Hand: Poetry in Song* by William Crofut, illustrated by Susan Crofut, they go hand in heart. The handsome volume contains 15 poems, most about nature and animals, arranged for children and adults to sing and play. Among the poems are such favorites as "In Just" by e. e. cummings; "The Chipmunk's Day," "The Mockingbird," and "The Bird of Night" by Randall Jarrell; and "Eletelephony" by Laura Richards. Musical arrangements by Kenneth Cooper and Glen Shattuck include a variety of instrumental possibilities—from piano to flute or the human voice. This 80-page symphony could lead children to set other poems to music, either those they find in books or ones they have composed.

Big, bountiful, bursting songbooks, such as the following four titles, will satisfy almost any class's urge for a group sing-along. Two volumes that will warm children in any weather are

The Fireside Songbook of Birds and Beasts, collected by Jane Yolen, with musical arrangements by Barbara Green and illustrated by Peter Parnall (a many-time Caldecott Honor Book winner), and *The Fireside Book of Fun and Game Songs*, collected by Marie Winn, with musical arrangements by Allan Miller. The first contains nearly 100 tunes, each prefaced with an introductory note that pays tribute to four-footed, feathery, and fishy creatures. The second is *the* book for camps, outings, bus rides, picnics, homes, and classrooms. Among the ten categories are action songs, involving clapping and snapping, pantomimes, follow-the-leader songs, rounds, and easy harmonies.

The Great Song Book: A Collection of Best Loved Songs in the English Language, edited by Timothy John, with music edited by Peter Hankey, is attractively designed with full-color illustrations throughout by Tomi Ungerer. The volume is divided into eight main sections featuring "Songs of Dance and Play," "Nursery Rhymes and Songs," as well as farmers, morning, fireside, folk, Christmas and evening songs, and lullabies. An index is included.

Lullabies and Night Songs, edited by William Engvick, with music by Alec Wilder and magnificent full-color illustrations by the incomparable Maurice Sendak, is as perfect now as when it first appeared in 1965. This is a must for any music-minded youngster, as well as any collector of beautiful volumes.

AND A ONE, AND A TWO . . .

Once the students' repertoires are well-rounded, help them plan a concert for another class, their whole grade, or even the entire school. First, let them brainstorm their own theme. Then, one group of volunteers might plan the program by taking a vote of class choices, later designing and duplicating copies of the works to be performed for the audience. Before the class band swings into practice, the children might want to schedule several vocal or instrumental solos. For added fun they could invite a guest accompanist—a teacher, a student from another class, a parent, or a grandparent—to perform.

Close the musicale by having everyone sing, sing, sing a popular song. Have a curtain call. And don't you forget to take a bow, too.

REFERENCES[1]

"American Songfest," a 16 mm. film produced by Weston Woods, Inc.

Bangs, Edward. *Yankee Doodle*, illustrated by Steven Kellogg. Parents' Magazine Press, 1976.

Bryan, Ashley. *Walk Together Children: Black American Spirituals*. Atheneum, 1974.

Crofut, William. *The Moon on the One Hand: Poetry in Song*. Atheneum, 1975.

Engvick, William. *Lullabies and Night Songs*, illustrated by Maurice Sendak. Harper & Row, 1965.

Faulhaber, Martha and Janet Underhill. *Music: Invent Your Own*. Whitman, 1974.

John, Timothy. *The Great Song Book: A Collection of Best Loved Songs in the English Language*. Doubleday. 1978.

Hawkinson, John, and Martha Faulhaber. *Music and Instruments for Children to Make*. Whitman, 1969.

———. *Rhythms, Music and Instruments to Make*. Whitman, 1970.

Langstaff, John. *Sweetly Sings the Donkey: Animal Rounds for Children to Sing and Play on Recorders*. Atheneum, 1976.

Quackenbush, Robert. *Clementine*. Lippincott, 1974.

———. *Go Tell Aunt Rhody*. Lippincott, 1973.

———. *The Man on the Flying Trapeze*. Lippincott, 1975.

———. *Old MacDonald Had a Farm*. Lippincott, 1972.

———. *Pop! Goes the Weasel* and *Yankee Doodle*. Lippincott, 1976.

———. *She'll Be Comin' 'Round the Mountain*. Lippincott, 1973.

———. *Skip to My Lou*. Lippincott, 1975.

———. *There'll Be A Hot Time in the Old Town Tonight*. Lippincott, 1974.

Seeger, Pete, and Charles Seeger. *The Foolish Frog*. Macmillan, 1973.

Spier, Peter. *The Star-Spangled Banner*. Doubleday, 1973.

Winn, Marie. *The Fireside Book of Fun and Game Songs*. Simon & Schuster, 1974.

Yolen, Jane. *The Fireside Songbook of Birds and Beasts*. Simon & Schuster, 1972.

[1]See Appendix for publishers' complete addresses.

Look! No words!

The best tribute wordless picture books can receive was offered by a first-grader with whom I worked. After she had thumbed through several such volumes, she exclaimed, "I like books like these. They say a lot without talking too much!"

Most people would be at a loss to better this pithy description of a genre that is almost 50 years old. As early as 1932, Ruth Carroll created the still widely popular, *What Whiskers Did,* a tale about a puppy who breaks his leash and runs away, only to face a series of dilemmas before returning to his young owner. Since then, many wordless books by a number of fine illustrators have appeared, including additional titles by Carroll such as *The Dolphin and the Mermaid,* published in 1974 —42 years after *What Whiskers Did*!

Using wordless books in your classroom can provide many opportunities for listening, discussing, writing, and dramatizing activities that stretch young minds and stimulate thinking among readers of all ages. Before you present wordless books to your students, take a moment to evaluate them according to one important criterion: The action and sequence must be clearly portrayed so that a child has no difficulty whatsoever in understanding the story.

IN THEIR OWN WORDS

Introducing wordless books in preprimary and primary classrooms is a classic way to encourage reading readiness. With no written vocabulary to wrestle with, youngsters can enjoy wonderful moments telling the tales in their own words. One of the best approaches is to have individual children or small groups look through a wordless book, relate their own versions, and compare their classmates' similarities and differences.

Two popular author/illustrators, both of whom have produced many wordless titles illlustrated in one and/or two colors are Mercer Mayer and Fernando Krahn. Mayer's very witty "Frog" series, beginning with *A Boy, a Dog and a Frog,* are available in many editions. Each of his volumes relates a warm adventure of an endearing frog and his many animal and human companions. Three other Mayer books you won't want to miss are *Ah-Choo, Hiccup,* and *Oops,* succinct titles for a series of disasters involving an elephant and a pair of hippos.

Krahn's work includes *Little Love Story,* a delightful tale about a boy's Valentine gift to a young girl; *The Self-Made Snowman,* in which a clump of snow rolls down a mountaintop and gradually takes on the appearance of an enormous and well-dressed snowman; and *The Biggest Christmas Tree on Earth,* a story about a girl who joins the forest animals in decorating their giant Christmas tree. Many children who live in areas where snow does not fall in winter will appreciate the warm-climate setting.

FULL-COLOR TREATMENTS

The past decade has also given rise to many full-color, lavishly produced wordless volumes, such as Peter Spier's 1978 Caldecott Award-winning *Noah's Ark* and *Changes, Changes* by Pat Hutchins. The latter is an imaginative flight of fancy about two wooden dolls who turn wooden blocks into whatever they choose. Both volumes are musts to stimulate children's visual awareness. An added bonus is that the two stories are available as filmstrips from Weston Woods, perfect for whole-class viewing and discussing.

Tana Hoban's wordless black-and-white nonfiction photographic works, such as *Look Again!* and *Count and See,* provide children with the opportunity to participate in both visual and language experiences. Her first title, done in full-color photography, *Is It Red? Is It Yellow? Is It Blue?* is a stunning adventure in color that paves the way for girls and boys to explore size, shape, and relationships.

Also, steer students to works by John S. Goodall. For younger children he has produced such titles as *The Midnight Adventures of Kelly, Dot, and Esmeralda,* about a koala bear, a doll, and a mouse who find adventure when they climb into a landscape painting, and two unique volumes designed with half-pages, *Creepy Castle* and *The Surprise Picnic.*

WORDLESS WONDERS FOR UPPER GRADERS

The delights of wordlessness are not limited to the very young. For older students there are more sophisticated and subtle volumes that invite close examination. By the way, wordless books can provide healthy exercise in such thinking skills as observing and inferring.

The Wonder Ring: A Fantasy in Silhouette by Holden Wetherbee features 136 hand-cut black-on-white silhouettes, capturing the mood and actions of a medieval boy's dream—from wood-chopping duties to a series of knightly adventures. A brief history of the silhouette is appended as well as instructions on how to make various types of cutouts.

Equally ingenious is *Anno's Journey* by Mitsumasa Anno. Meticulously rendered full-color watercolor paintings relate the story of the author's travels throughout northern Europe and his impressions of the land, the people, and their heritage. Astute lookers can find a multitude of happenings on each double-page spread, including details from paintings by Renoir and Seurat, children playing games, characters from "Sesame Street," literary figures (such as Pinocchio and Don Quixote), and even Beethoven sitting at a window. They will have to look hard, but the visual search will be well worth the effort.

Goodall has also used the technique of including half-pages in two volumes for older lookers, too: *An Edwardian Summer* recreates the life of an English village during Edwardian times; and *The Story of an English Village* depicts the changes that take place in an English village as it grows from a clearing in medieval times to a bustling modern town of the twentieth century. Both feature his exquisite full-color paintings.

A HAMSTER'S FOLLY

All ages will enjoy the antics of *Max* by Giovannetti. In a series of black-and-white cartoon incidents, Max, a beguiling hamster, displays his penchant for folly in such human activities as blow-drying his hair, having trouble with the ink in a fountain pen, and learning to ski. Having students create captions for Max's adventures is one good follow-up to "reading" about them. Or you can cut out the words in your students' favorite cartoon strips and ask them for suggestions on what the characters might be saying. (Many times their ideas are funnier than the originals!) This activity also reinforces dialogue-writing and the proper use of quotation marks.

After you introduce wordless books, your students might like to create their own series of wordless incidents via a wide variety of art techniques, such as collage, watercolors, pen-and-ink drawings, and silhouettes. They can present them to lower-grade classes or place them in the school library for all to view.

So much can be said without words. The plots, characters, settings, and feelings may be silent, but they convey voluble messages at every turn of the page.

REFERENCES[1]

Anno, Mitsumasa. *Anno's Journey.* Collins + World, 1977.
Carroll, Ruth. *The Dolphin and the Mermaid.* Walck, 1974.
——. *What Whiskers Did.* Macmillan, 1932; Scholastic paperback.
Giovannetti. *Max.* Atheneum, 1976.
Goodall, John S. *An Edwardian Summer.* Atheneum, 1976.
——. *Creepy Castle.* Atheneum, 1974.
——. *The Midnight Adventures of Kelly, Dot, and Esmeralda.* Atheneum, 1975.
——. *The Story of an English Village.* Atheneum, 1979.
——. *Spring Picnic.* Atheneum, 1976.
Hoban, Tana. *Count and See.* Macmillan, 1971.
——. *Is It Red? Is It Yellow? Is It Blue?* Greenwillow, 1978.
——. *Look Again!* Macmillan, 1971
Hutchins, Pat. *Changes, Changes.* Macmillan, 1971.

[1]See Appendix for publishers' complete addresses.

Krahn, Fernando. *The Biggest Christmas Tree on Earth.* Little, Brown, 1978.

———. *Little Love Story.* Lippincott, 1976.

———. *The Self-Made Snowman.* Lippincott, 1974.

Mayer, Mercer. *A Boy, a Dog, and a Frog.* Dial, 1971; also available in paperback.

———. *Ah Choo.* Dial, 1976; also available in paperback.

———. *Hiccup.* Dial, 1976; also available in paperback.

———. *Oops.* Dial, 1977; also available in paperback.

Spier, Peter. *Noah's Ark.* Doubleday, 1977.

Wetherbee, Holden. *The Wonder Ring: A Fantasy in Silhouette.* Doubleday, 1978; also available in paperback.

Relooking at classics

Janey, a 10-year-old neighbor, is an exceptional reader and lover of books. She haunts libraries, librarians, teachers—anyone who "knows books"—for her next reading adventure. Well-versed in fine children's literature, she has devoured title after title by many of today's writers.

In one of our casual book conversations, I asked Janey if she had ever read *Alice's Adventures in Wonderland* by Lewis Carroll. She flinched, answering tersely, "Alice in Wonderland? That's a baby book! I read it when I was a baby."

"How about *Pinocchio* (by Carlo Collodi)? Did you ever read that?" I posed.

"No, but I saw the movie about five times. That's a baby story, too. It's stupid!" she answered.

All of the wishes, dreams, and aspirations of childhood and the beautifully written text contained in these and all classic works of literature went "down the hole" for Janey faster than Alice and the rabbit did in Carroll's masterpiece. By the time they reach Janey's age, many children feel that they have "read" the classics. In part, this is due to inferior motion-picture treatments and the many watered-down versions—cheap both in price and content—that are introduced to girls and boys long before they are ready for them. If your students literally "put down" the best that children's literature has to offer, encourage them to take another look.

WHAT IS OLD?

A classic is often associated with age and time, but many children have difficulty understanding these concepts. So, before getting them on the classics path, sound out some classroom opinions on what "old" is. Some of the children's immediate responses may center on a grandparent who is in his or her 50s or a neighbor who has just turned 30! To help students think of "old" in a different light, you might ask, "What is the oldest thing your parents or grandparents own?"

Elaborate on this discussion by planning an Antiques Day in the classroom. Have the children or their parents bring in their oldest, most prized possessions and talk about the age of the items. A drawing will make a good substitute if the antique itself cannot leave home.

Viewing old coins, utensils, or family albums in this manner can pave the way for a discussion of classic stories. For example, ask the children to bring their favorite books to class. Open one to the first few pages to show the children where they can find the copyright date and printing history. This information usually includes the date of the first edition, the publisher, and the dates of subsequent editions. What is the oldest copyright date that the children can find?

Middle-graders, as well as college students I have worked with, are often amazed to learn that many of the books they are now reading or grew up with were written and published during the nineteenth and early twentieth centuries. This kind of discovery can help the children better understand the lasting quality and universal appeal of classic books. Some of the better-known titles are *A Christmas Carol* by Charles Dickens (1843), *The Fairy Tales of Hans Christian Andersen* (1846), *Alice's Adventures in Wonderland* (1865), *Little Women* by Louisa May Alcott (1868), and *The Wind in the Willows* by Kenneth Grahame (1908). Scan your library's shelves for numerous hardcover and paperbound editions of these titles.

SHARING AND COMPARING

The world of picture books provides a bounty of tales in editions that children will enjoy, love, and remember forever.

Among them are fairy tales, folklore, and nursery rhymes that have endured the test of time.

Some unique editions are those interpreted by the contemporary author and artist Paul Galdone. His retellings of well-loved stories are done in full-color illustrations that spring up to the reader's eyes as soon as each page is turned. Among them are perennial favorites such as *The Gingerbread Boy, The Three Billy Goats Gruff, The Three Bears, The Three Little Pigs,* and *Three Aesop Fox Fables.*

Encouraging children to seek out various versions of the same story to compare will exercise library skills and give research a new purpose. For example, Galdone's *Puss in Boots* might be read, observed, and compared to the same title interpreted by Marcia Brown, Charles Perrault and Hans Fischer, or M. Jean Craig.

Reluctant readers in the middle-and upper-grades can also explore the classics via a comparison approach. For example, as children pore through varied editions of a folktale such as *Stone Soup,* ask them if they can spot similarities and differences in characterization, plot, and artwork. In Marcia Brown's rendition of *Stone Soup,* French soldiers trick villagers into providing them with the ingredients for a delicious soup that they claim they can make from three stones. Margot Zemach has illustrated a Swedish version, *Nail Soup,* adapted from the text by Nils Djurkly. A Russian version, "Hatchet Gruel," appears in *Three Rolls and One Doughnut: Fables from Russia,* edited by Mirra Ginsburg and illustrated by Anita Lobel. And in a paperback edition of *Stone Soup* by Ann McGovern, illustrated by Nola Langner, there's still another twist to the tale due to the greed of an old woman.

Middle-graders can get their creative juices flowing by writing parodies or satires based on classic literature themes. Talis Byers, an instructor at the Park Vista Elementary School in Opelousas, Louisiana, has students retread old tales by adding new twists—relating modern technology and discoveries to original story lines and characters. Among the concoctions students came up with was a retelling of *Pinocchio,* called "The Adventures of the Boy with the Bionic Nose," and *Henny Penny,* whereby the original falling sky became an unidentified flying object and retitled, "Henny's Close Encounter." My own students have taken such tales as *Rumpelstiltskin* and *Sleeping Beauty* and have changed the locales to the Old and

Wild West. New titles that emerged were "Rumpelspurskin," and "The Sleeping Deb." Try such titles as "Cinderella Goes Disco," or "Snow White and the Seven Giants," to get students started on their very own encounters.

Folktales and fairy tales such as these provide a rich literary stock for creative dramatics and playwriting. One enterprising sixth grader set Carroll's wonderful verse, "Beautiful Soup," from *Alice's Adventure in Wonderland,* to music to enhance the poem's enactment by the class for younger students. A fitting climax to their production was a chorus of 30 children singing the verse.[1]

Better readers might report on various illustrators interpretations of a full-length book by looking at different volumes. *Little Women,* as illustrated by Jessie Wilcox Smith or Tasha Tudor, might be used as a start.

All children's classics provide rich material for other language arts and arts activities, too. Students can create dioramas, murals, or life-sized figures of favorite characters and compose poems or plan compositions on classic book themes. To round out a classics project, encourage students to choose, predict, and vote for contemporary works that *they* feel just might become future favorites.

THE USES OF CLASSICS

Sound advice regarding when and how to use classics is offered by Charlotte S. Huck in "Understanding Children and Literature," the first chapter of *Children's Literature in the Elementary School.* Two other professional references provide more guidance: *Children's Classics,* a 16-page paperbound essay by Alice M. Jordan, contains a list of recommended editions by Paul Heins (available from The Horn Book, Inc.); *The Uses of Enchantment: The Meaning and Importance of Fairy Tales* by Bruno Bettelheim is a thought-provoking psychological study that deserves a prominent place on every school and public library shelf.

Not all children are ready to tackle the classics. But with some preparation and thought, you can help them become more appreciative readers and lovers of these timeless works.

[1]For complete text of the poem, see page 149.

POSTSCRIPT

After reading my copy of *Alice,* Janey returned the book and left the following note:

Dear Mr. Hopkins:
   I thought I read *Alice* until I read it. There's more to it than just her falling down the hole. It's the best book I ever read.
Your friend,
Janey

REFERENCES[2,3]

Alcott, Louisa May. *Little Women,* illustrated by Tasha Tudor. Collins + World, 1969.

———. *Little Women,* illustrated by Jessie Wilcox Smith. Little, Brown, 1968.

Andersen, Hans Christian. *The Fairy Tales of Hans Christian Andersen.*[3]

Bettleheim, Bruno. *The Uses of Enchantment: The Meaning and Importance of Fairy Tales.* Knopf, 1976; also available in paperback.

Brown, Marcia. *Puss in Boots.* Scribner, 1952.

———. *Stone Soup.* Scribner, 1947.

Carroll, Lewis. *Alice's Adventures in Wonderland.*[3]

Collodi, Carlo. *Pinocchio.*[3]

Craig, M. Jean. *Puss in Boots.* Scholastic paperback.

Dickens, Charles. *A Christmas Carol.*[3]

Galdone, Paul. *The Gingerbread Boy.* Seabury, 1975.

———. *Puss in Boots.* Seabury, 1975.

———. *Three Aesop Fox Fables.* Seabury, 1975.

———. *The Three Bears.* Seabury, 1972.

———.*The Three Billy Goats Gruff.* Seabury, 1973.

———. *The Three Little Pigs.* Seabury, 1972.

Ginsburg, Mirra. *Three Rolls and One Doughnut: Fables from Russia.* Dial, 1970.

Grahame, Kenneth. *The Wind in the Willows.* Scribner, 1908.

Huck, Charlotte S. *Children's Literature in the Elementary School,* 3d ed. Holt, Rinehart and Winston, 1979.

Jordon, Alice M. *Children's Classics.* The Horn Book, Inc., paperbound.

McGovern, Ann. *Stone Soup.* Scholastic paperback.

Perrault, Charles, and Hans Fischer. *Puss in Boots.* Harcourt, 1959.

Zemach, Margot. *Nail Soup.* Follett, 1964.

[2]See Appendix: Publishers' Complete Addresses.
[3]Available in many hardbound and paperback editions.

16

Variety:
The spice of life, language, and literature

One afternoon, an 11-year-old boy presented me with his very astute observation on the nature of words.

"It's amazing," he said, "that every single word written in the English language is made up from only 26 letters of the alphabet!"

It is a marvel that the diversity of our language rests on those 26 letters, the tools of every writer. Letter combinations form words; words turn into sentences; sentences into paragraphs; paragraphs into books of every kind. Exploring this variety of titles, through various genre of children's books, can add excitement to reading and heighten students' awareness of the elements of fine writing.

You are the best judge of the types of books that appeal to your students. Some girls and boys have well-rounded reading diets, a few may dabble, and others may stick to one favorite type, such as biography, fantasy, adventure, or nonfiction accounts of the animal world. But whatever students' reading tastes are, you can motivate them to sample and enjoy other areas.

For example, you might plan a "Galaxy of Reading" bulletin board display. Students can design paper suns and planets of different colors and place them under this caption, labeling each sun a different genre. As children read books from any of the categories featured on the bulletin board, they can record the title and author along with their name on a planet of the appropriate sun.

To focus attention on the language an author uses—an important aspect in learning to appreciate different kinds of books—place a large, brown envelope near the door and ask the children to drop in cards on which they have copied a favorite descriptive passage, the title, and author. When they line up for gym, lunch, or dismissal, have one or two students reach in and read a card. This activity will help them to decide which book they might like to take out next from the library.

Descriptive passages can also be used for a "Guess My Category" quiz game. You or a student can read aloud sections from different genre and have the whole class or small groups guess the type. Or distribute duplicated sheets of paper divided into squares with the name of a different genre placed in each one. Read each passage, title, and author aloud and have the children write the title and author in the square in which they think the book belongs. For example, in which categories would the following passages fit?

"Miyax pushed back the hood of her sealskin parka and looked at the Arctic sun. It was a yellow disc in a lime-green sky, the colors of six o'clock in the evening and the time when the wolves awake."

—from *Julie of the Wolves*
by Jean Craighead George, page 5.

"In 1706 in Boston, Benjamin Franklin was born with just one life. From the beginning, he was full of brilliant ideas and humor. As he grew, he put them to use. So he became a man of many lives."

—from *The Many Lives of
Benjamin Franklin* by
Aliki, page 5.

"One day when things were dull in Hell, the Devil fished around in his bag of disguises, dressed himself as a fairy godmother, and came up into the World to find someone to bother."

—From *The Devil's Storybook*
by Natalie Babbitt, page 3.

SEARCHING FOR LANGUAGE

The effective use of parts of speech, metaphors, similes, and alliteration is as basic to the writer's craft as a sleuth is to a mystery story or a haunted house to a gothic novel. To help children become more conscious of these elements, have them collect and copy down examples in their notebooks under appropriate headings and then discuss them.

Poetry, of course, is filled with descriptive language. Metaphors can be found in many poems, such as "The River Is A Piece of Sky" from *The Reason for the Pelican* by John Ciardi, illustrated by Madeleine Gekire; "Some say the sun is a golden earring," by Natalia M. Belting in *Piping Down the Valleys Wild,* edited by Nancy Larrick and illustrated by Ellen Raskin; and "The Moon's the North Wind's Cooky" by Vachel Lindsay in *The Moon's the North Wind's Cooky: Night Poems*, selected and illustrated by Susan Russo. A simile comparing snails to tiny thumbs and fingernails appears in the poem, "Ants and Sailboats," by David McCord in *One At A Time: His Collected Poems for the Young*, illustrated by Henry B. Kane.

Of course, alliteration abounds in tongue-twisters: "Peter Piper picked a peck of pickled peppers."

To demonstrate how parts of speech, such as adjectives, are used by writers to draw word pictures, write the word *dog* on the chalkboard. Ask each child to call out the first adjective that comes to mind. A class of 30 students might easily yield 30 different adjectives to describe a kennel full of canines. Then read aloud the opening lines of Irene Rutherford McLeod's poem, "Lone Dog," a selection that abounds with adjectives describing a well-seasoned hunting dog and includes such adjectives as lean, keen, wild, lone, rough, tough, and so on. The poem appears in *To Look At Any Thing*, selected by Lee Bennett Hopkins with photographs by John Earl, as well as in the above-mentioned *Piping Down the Valleys Wild* by Larrick. Discuss with children how each adjective successfully adds to and slightly changes the image of the animal.

The most eloquent language would be a hopeless mess without punctuation marks. To emphasize their importance, offer *On Your Marks: A Package of Punctuation* by Richard Armour (with a foreword by Ogden Nash), a treasure trove of poems about the dots, curves, and lines that clarify the meaning of words. Included are specific verses on various punctuation marks such as "The Period," "The Comma," "The Apostrophe," and "The Semicolon." Poems about punctuation also appear in Eve Merriam's *Finding A Poem*, illustrated by Seymour Chwast. They include "Markings: The Period," "Markings: The Question Mark," "Markings: The Exclamation Point," "Markings: The Comma," and "Markings: The Semicolon," followed by a concrete poem titled, "Showers, Clearing Later in the Day," designed with exclamation points, asterisks, and periods.

A quarterly publication that you will welcome for its sound ideas on using different kinds of children's books is *The Web* (*Wonderfully Exciting Books*), coedited by Charlotte S. Huck and Janet Hickman. In addition to reviewing books and suggesting ways they can be used in the classroom, each issue features a double-paged "web" that centers on a particular title and theme from which extend related activities and book suggestions. For example, one issue focused on "Surprises: A Web of Possibilities," giving ideas and book titles to use to spark such topics as "Party Surprises," "Surprises in Nature," "Visual Surprises," and books with "Surprise Endings."

This "wonderfully exciting" source also includes children's reactions to books—one of the few places where young voices *are* heard from. Subscriptions are available for $4.00 per year, by writing to *The Web*, The Ohio State University, Room 200, Ramseyer Hall, 20 West Woodruff, Columbus, Ohio, 43210.

REFERENCES[1]

Aliki. *The Many Lives of Benjamin Franklin*. Prentice-Hall, 1977.

Armour, Richard. *On Your Marks: A Package of Punctuation*. McGraw-Hill, 1969.

Babbitt, Natalie. *The Devil's Storybook*. Farrar, Straus, 1974; Bantam paperback.

Ciardi, John. *The Reason for the Pelican*. Lippincott, 1959.

George, Jean Craighead. *Julie of the Wolves*. Harper & Row, 1972; also available in paperback.

Hopkins, Lee Bennett, ed. *To Look At Any Thing*. Harcourt, 1978.

Larrick, Nancy, ed. *Piping Down the Valleys Wild*. Delacorte, 1968; Dell paperback.

McCord, David. *One At A Time: His Collected Poems for the Young*. Little, Brown, 1977.

Merriam, Eve. *Finding A Poem*. Atheneum, 1970.

Russo, Susan, ed. *The Moon's the North Wind's Cooky: Night Poems*. Lothrop, 1979.

[1]See Appendix for publishers' complete addresses.

PART IV

The Seasons

Celebrate December with books

No matter what grade you teach or where, December is a time of celebration, a month-long stretch when children of all ages burst with thoughts of wintertime frolic, colorful holiday feasts, and merrymaking. It is also the first major break since school began last September! You can easily capitalize on the season's excitement, steering girls and boys into thinking deeply about its unique qualities and the meaning of its two most well-known holidays—Christmas and Hanukkah.

How does winter "speak" to your students? Through chilly, blustery days? With snowpacked sidewalks? Or does your area sport a sun-filled winter? Whatever the season brings, the wonder of winter—sparkling snow, frosty air, fragile snowflakes—fascinate children and adults alike.

To most children, the first days of December mean the beginning of winter, even though the season doesn't officially start until December 21. Introduce "ol' man winter" to your younger readers via books with winter themes that have won the Caldecott Award—*White Snow, Bright Snow* by Alvin Tresselt, illustrated by Roger Duvoisin; *The Big Snow* by Berta and Elmer Hader; *Nine Days to Christmas* by Marie Hall Ets and Aurora Labastida; *Baboushka and the Three Kings* by Ruth Robbins, illustrated by Nicolas Sidjakov; and *The Snowy Day* written and illustrated by Ezra Jack Keats. Hearing these delights and poring over the illustrations might spark girls and boys to illustrate favorite winter scenes for a bulletin board display.

CHRISTMAS

Let winter "speak" with holidays, too. Christmas is an important time of year for Christians; it is a day that marks the birth of Jesus Christ nearly 2000 years ago. The holiday is celebrated in a variety of ways from family to family and country to country. Two particularly helpful, easy-to-read reference volumes about Christmas are *Christmas Feasts and Festivals* by Lillie Patterson, illustrated by Clift Schule; and *Christmas,* written and illustrated by Barbara Cooney.

Student volunteers might collect other nonfiction books about the holiday by visiting school or public libraries. The children might also investigate home libraries, which are often storehouses of fascinating materials. When sufficient materials are on hand, in-class research can begin. Many children may be quite surprised to learn that some of the customs we associate with Christmas were actually practiced long before the birth of Christ.

Ancient people living in the Northern Hemisphere worshipped the sun. As days grew shorter during the winter months, people feared that the evil powers of darkness were coming to kill all living things, so they kindled lights and fires to help the sun god. The Persians lighted fires to praise their god of light, Mithra, and the Egyptians honored Isis, mother of Horusand, the sun god. Early Native Americans also invested great reverence in the sun as the source of all light and life. This belief is elegantly portrayed in a Pueblo tale, *Arrow to the Sun,* adapted and illustrated in glorious full-color by Gerald McDermott, winner of the 1975 Caldecott Award. The book is also available as an animated film from Texture Films.

The triumph of light and warmth over darkness and cold still prevails as an important part of the Christmas celebration. The yule log is traditionally lit on Christmas Eve, adding warmth and light to the holiday celebration. Evergreens, "the plants that do not die," are decked with bangles and lights, recalling the ancients' belief that the evergreen held some of the sun god's magic and would ensure the sun's return.

The holiday is rich with other symbols, too. Students might use *Holly, Reindeer and Colored Lights: The Story of the*

Christmas Symbols by Edna Barth to delve into the meaning of some of them. Written in a simple prose, the book traces similarities between Christmas and earlier pagan feasts. Illustrations are by Ursula Arndt.

Compile the children's research into a "Christmas Signs and Symbols" booklet. And, of course, don't let the month go by without sharing some lively Christmas tales. For younger readers, there are many holiday delights.

Arthur's Christmas Cookies, written and illustrated by Lillian Hoban, tells of Arthur a chimpanzee, and his friends who make inedible presents. *The Twelve Days of Christmas* is a popular old folk tune made gloriously new with Brian Wildsmith's unmistakably brilliant artwork. Students could follow up by learning the tune and caroling it to another class. *Father Christmas,* written and illustrated in full-color pictures à la comic book format by Raymond Briggs, is about a grumpy but kindly Father Christmas who dreams of sunny, tropical holidays. *How Santa Claus Had a Long and Difficult Journey Delivering His Presents* is a wordless book by Fernando Krahn which youngsters will enjoy adding their very own story lines to.

Older readers will revel in the *The Best Christmas Pageant Ever* by Barbara Robinson, a very funny and touching tale about six children who take over the school's annual Christmas pageant.

All ages will enjoy the beautiful edition of Hans Christian Andersen's *The Fir Tree,* with Nancy Ekholm Burkert's illustrations in black-and-white and full color.

A fun idea to use with children is to post on a bulletin board display how "Merry Christmas" is said in a variety of languages. Have students match the countries to the languages:

Aferihia Pa—Ashanti
Glaedelig Jul—Danish
Joyeux Nöel—French
Frohliche Weinachten—German
Kala Christougenna—Greek
Buon Natale—Italian
S Rhozhdyestvom Khristovym—Russian
Feliz Navidad—Spanish.

Encourage children to discover how to say "Merry Christmas" in other languages, too. Parents might be a valuable resource for this. Greetings could be assembled into a "December Dictionary." Underneath the bulletin board or close to it, have a table covered with brightly colored paper or a class-designed seasonal tablecloth. The display could include various seasonal and holiday symbols, some of which could be made by the students. Books the children have gathered from research and class-made booklets might be displayed, also.

HANUKKAH

Hanukkah, or the Festival of Lights, lasts eight days. It begins on the twenty-fifth day of the Hebrew month of Kislev. On the Roman calendar, this falls at the end of November or some time during the month of December. The holiday is a joyous occasion commemorating the Hebrew victory over Syria's oppressive King Antiochus, in which the Maccabees recaptured the temple of Jerusalem.

The menorah, a candelabrum, is an important symbol of the event. The menorah has nine cups for candles. Eight candles represent the eight days the oil burned during the first Hanukkah. Hebrew legend states that the Maccabees were miraculously able to burn one day's oil supply for eight days once their temple was cleansed of Antiochus' pagan statues. The candlelight reminds the Jewish people of their fight to pray to God in their own way. The ninth cup holds the shamas candle. *Shamas* means *servant* in Hebrew. Each night the shamas is lit first and then used to light the other candles. One candle is lit each night until all eight burn brightly. Children receive small gifts on each of the eight days, sing songs, and play games.

A top-like toy, the dreidel, might be shown to the children. It is closely associated with the holiday, and children will be fascinated to discover its role in the Hanukkah ritual. On each side is one Hebrew letter: Nun, or N; Gimel, or G; Hei, or H; Shin, or Sh. These are the first letters of the Hebrew words *nes godal hayah sham,* meaning "a great miracle happened there." Several children can demonstrate to the class how to play dreidel. Each player has a chance to spin the dreidel, and how it falls determines the outcome of the game.

Many children confuse Hanukkah with Christmas. This is a good time of year to have individuals or small groups plan a report on the significance of each of the holidays to share with the class.

Younger readers can find out more about the symbols and customs of the holiday in *Hanukkah* by Norma Simon, illustrated by Symeon Shimin; and *The Hanukkah Story,* written and illustrated by Marilyn Hirsh. Upper-graders will enjoy *The Story of Hanukkah* by Betty Morrow, illustrated by Howard Simon; and *Chanukah,* by Howard Greenfeld, designed by Bea Feitler.

Interesting facts can be compiled into a "Hanukkah Hand-booklet." The students can design the booklet in the shape of a dreidel or some other Hanukkah symbol.

POETRY PEG

The poetry that has been sparked by December celebrations is as rich and varied as the season's holidays themselves. Good resources to have on hand any time of the year are *Skip Around the Year* by Aillen Fisher, illustrated by Gioia Fiammenghi; and *More Poetry for Holidays,* an anthology selected by Nancy Larrick, illustrated by Harold Berson. You will find "Light the Festive Candles," a poem written especially to celebrate Hanukkah in Fisher's delightful book, and you can usher Christmas in with four special poems—"Suddenly," "First Gifts," "Country Christmas," and "Christmas Candles." Three Hanukkah poems, including one written by the children at the Jewish Children's School in Philadelphia, Pennsylvania, can be found in Larrick's collection, as well as five selections for Christmas.

Twenty poems appear in Lee Bennett Hopkins' *Sing Hey for Christmas Day!* including works by e. e. cummings, Langston Hughes, and Christina Rossetti. The volume is illustrated in green-and-white illustrations by Laura Jean Allen.

Celebrate December with books—it is such a wonderful way to end the old year and to begin looking forward to the new one.

REFERENCES[1]

Andersen, Hans Christian. *The Fir Tree.* Harper & Row, 1970.
Barth, Edna. *Holly, Reindeer and Colored Lights: The Story of the Christmas Symbols.* Seabury, 1971.

[1]See Appendix for publishers' complete addresses.

Briggs, Raymond. *Father Christmas.* Coward McCann, 1973.

Cooney, Barbara. *Christmas.* Crowell, 1967.

Ets, Marie Hall, and Aurora Labastida. *Nine Days To Christmas.* Viking, 1959.

Fisher, Aileen. *Skip Around the Year.* Crowell, 1967.

Greenfeld, Howard. *Chanukah.* Holt, Rinehart and Winston, 1976.

Hader, Berta, and Elmer Hader. *The Big Snow.* Macmillan, 1948.

Hirsh, Marilyn. *The Hanukkah Story.* Bonim, 1977.

Hoban, Lillian. *Arthur's Christmas Cookies.* Harper & Row, 1972.

Hopkins, Lee Bennett. *Sing Hey for Christmas Day!* Harcourt, 1975.

Keats, Ezra Jack. *The Snowy Day.* Viking, 1962; Scholastic paperback.

Krahn, Fernando. *How Santa Claus Had a Long and Difficult Journey Delivering His Presents.* Delacorte, 1970; also available in paperback.

Larrick, Nancy. *More Poetry for Holidays.* Garrard, 1973; Scholastic paperback.

McDermott, Gerald. *Arrow to the Sun.* Viking, 1974.

Morrow, Betty. *The Story of Hanukkah.* Harvey House, 1964.

Patterson, Lillie. *Christmas Feasts and Festivals.* Garrard, 1968.

Robbins, Ruth. *Baboushka and the Three Kings.* Parnassus Press, 1960.

Robinson, Barbara. *The Best Christmas Pageant Ever.* Harper & Row, 1972; Avon paperback.

Simon, Norma. *Hanukkah.* Crowell, 1966.

Tresselt, Alvin. *White Snow, Bright Snow.* Lothrop, 1947.

Wildsmith, Brian. *The Twelve Days of Christmas.* Watts, 1972.

Happy Birthdays

Among the most important days in any school year are students' birthdays. Whether they are marking their first birthday in school or are celebrating the ripe old age of 12, children want *their* day to be remembered and shared with others.

September is the perfect time to chart birthdates as well as the children's other vital statistics. Have them list their names and dates of birth on 12 oaktag charts labeled "September" through "August" or on the pages of a large calendar. The charts can be as simple or as complex as you and your students care to make them. They are helpful reminders of whose big days are about to come up—occasions that can be a special part of classroom activities. For example, you can set aside a small bulletin board or a corner of a large one for birthday "Children of the Month" to design and decorate. This will give them a chance to tell about themselves through creative writing, drawings, or photographs that describe their interests in sports, television shows, hobbies, pets, and favorite books.

An attractive project used in one primary-grade classroom was a "Birthday Train." Different colored pieces of oaktag were labeled and connected to form a month-by-month set of railroad cars, which the children filled in with their names and birthdates. Similar bulletin board ideas that can be used to reflect current classroom interests are 12 rocket ships heading for "The Birthday Planet"; 12 stars attached to the board or hung from the ceiling to make up "A Sky of Birthdays"; individual construction-paper flowers inscribed with the child's name and birthdate and attached to stick stems to bloom in "A Garden of Birthdays." Small photographs of each child pasted on the rocket ships, stars, or flowers add to the total effect.

At the end of the school year, you might want to plan a picnic celebration for those children whose birthdays fall during summer vacation. This is also a nice time to honor those students who came into your class during the year, after their birthdays had passed.

READ ME A BIRTHDAY

To introduce primary graders to books about birthdays, discuss titles, authors, and illustrators, and remind the class that school and public libraries have many stories and poems on birthday themes. Below are several popular selections for young readers and listeners.

A Birthday for Frances by Russell Hoban, illustrated by Lillian Hoban, depicts Frances's mixed feelings as the beguiling badger bunch celebrates little sister Gloria's birthday. In *The Birthday Goat* by Nancy Dingman Watson, with full-color illustrations by Wendy Watson, Paulette chooses to celebrate her big day by going with her family to a carnival. Everything goes well until Baby Souci is kidnapped. Designed in comic-book style, the volume uses frames with dialogue printed in balloons. *Happy Birthday to You!,* written and illustrated by Dr. Seuss, takes place in the land of Katroo, the only place in the nation where Birthday Birds grow and are trained by The Katroo Happy Birthday Asso-see-eye-ation. Another charming tale to share is "Birthday Soup" in the now-classic *Little Bear,* an "I Can Read" book by Else Holmelund Minarik, with pictures by Maurice Sendak.

A wonderful resource of birthday lore is offered in *The Golden Happy Birthday Book,* compiled by Barbara Shook Hazen. Featured are stories and poems by such authors as Margaret Wise Brown, Edith Thacher Hurd, and Charlotte Zolotow. Also included is information on birthday observances in other lands, birthstones and flowers, riddles, puzzles, jokes, games, tricks, and ideas for making party favors, invitations, and decorations. Illustrations are by Rosalyn Schanzer.

ON THE DAY I WAS BORN

An intriguing birthday activity for the middle and upper grades provides a fun-filled introduction to the subject of probability. Ask each child to poll at least 30 people on when their birthdays are. Predict that in most polls the birthdays of at least two people will match. According to probability theory, there is a better than two-to-one chance that two people in any group of 30 will have the same birthdate. The children will be surprised and delighted when your prediction comes true.

Many students, particularly upper graders, also enjoy doing research on the famous people who share their birthday or the special events that occurred on that date. Two references providing a wealth of such information are *Do You Know What Day Tomorrow Is?: A Teacher's Almanac* by Lee Bennett Hopkins and Misha Arenstein, and *The Teacher's Almanack: A Complete Guide to Every Day of the School Year* by Dana Newman. The Hopkins/Arenstein volume offers a miscellany of information about people, sports, history, the fine arts, science, and other topics covering events from September through August. To complement the facts, an appropriate poem for each month and many fiction and nonfiction book suggestions are included for further reading by students who are intrigued by particular subjects.

Newman's book spans from September through June and features calendar listings of important dates as well as recipes, games, riddles, and experiments to tie in with specific holidays and events.

POETRY PEG

If they want to, children can memorize and recite a poem, making this a different type of birthday present. For unusual selections of birthday verse, students can consult "Birthdays" in *Callooh! Callay!: Holiday Poems for Young Readers* and "Birth, Birthdays and Christenings" in *O Frabjous Day: Poetry for Holidays and Special Occasions,* both edited by Myra Cohn Livingston. A worldwide range of poets' work appears in these two volumes from the contemporary thoughts of such American writers as David McCord and Robert Frost to the voices of poets from Spain, Israel, China, and Japan.

REACHING OUT

Sharing the joy of special days can extend far beyond the classroom. For example, if there is a nursing home or senior citizen organization in your area, it would be a great learning experience to have girls and boys "adopt" a grandparent. As the children discover birthdates of their new friends, they can help them celebrate in special ways by making original greeting cards or arts and crafts gifts.

Another idea is to have students do research to find out who are the oldest members of the community. By inviting these men and women to class and preparing advance questions, girls and boys will glean a great deal of firsthand information about the past, such as childhood experiences, inventions that appeared during their lifetimes, and historical events which they remember living through.

ROUSING CHORUS

Naturally, no birthday would be complete without singing the traditional "Happy Birthday to You," written in 1934 by two American sisters, Mildred J. and Patty S. Hill. The song is sung all over the world in almost every language. If you have children who speak a foreign language, ask them to sing or teach the lyrics to the entire class.

Make birthdays special times for all. And don't forget to celebrate yours with the class as well!

REFERENCES[1]

Hazen, Barbara Shook. *The Golden Happy Birthday Book.* Western, 1976.

Hoban, Russell. *A Birthday for Frances.* Harper & Row, 1968; also available in paperback.

Hopkins, Lee Bennett, and Misha Arenstein. *Do You Know What Day Tomorrow Is?: A Teacher's Almanac.* Scholastic/Citation, 1975; also available in paperback.

Livingston, Myra Cohn. *Callooh! Callay!: Holiday Poems for Young Readers.* Atheneum, 1978.

[1]See Appendix for publishers' complete addresses

————. *O Frabjous Day: Poetry for Holidays and Special Occasions.*
    Atheneum, 1977.
Minarik, Else Holmelund. *Little Bear.* Harper & Row, 1957; also avail-
    able in paperback.
Newman, Dana. *The Teacher's Almanack: A Complete Guide to Every
    Day of the School Year.* The Center for Applied Research, 1973.
Seuss, Dr. *Happy Birthday To You!* Random House, 1959.
Watson, Nancy Dingman. *The Birthday Goat.* Crowell, 1974; also
    available in paperback.

Halloween and when it's over:
Boo, shiver and tingle tales

For many people, October conjures up thoughts of assorted creatures—real and imagined. It is synonymous with Halloween, one of the oldest and most colorful celebration in the world. The holiday began with the Celts, who held a festival called Samhain, meaning "end of summer," and evolved into what we now know as trick-or-treat night, when witches and wizards and even space-age astronauts seek sweets from friends and neighbors.

HISTORICAL HALLOWEEN

Early in the month, ask for volunteer Halloween researchers to collect Halloween history facts. They can share them later with classmates or other classes as part of an October 31 class or school fête. To help students with their research, you might include the following titles in a spooky book display.

Two volumes particularly suited for younger readers are *Halloween,* written and illustrated by Helen Borten; and *Halloween* by Lillie Patterson, illustrated by Gil Meret. Both books briefly tell of Halloween customs and how the holiday came to be. Older readers will reap a great deal of information from *Witches, Pumpkins and Grinning Ghosts: The Story of Halloween Symbols* by Edna Barth, illustrated by Ursula Arndt.

Add poems to the festivities, too. *Hey-How for Halloween*

contains 22 verses for children of all ages selected by Lee Bennett Hopkins, paying tribute to the spine-tingling season. Poems by such well-known writers as e. e. cummings, Carl Sandburg, Myra Cohn Livingston, and May Justus range from the scary to the whimsical. The book is illustrated in black-and-white drawings by Janet McCaffery.

Witch Poems, edited by Daisy Wallace, features 18 selections including verse by Karla Kuskin, Felice Holman, and Eleanor Farjeon. The spook-filled black-and-white illustrations are by Trina Schart Hyman. Poet Jack Prelutsky offers 13 original selections in *It's Halloween,* illustrated in color by Marilyn Hafner.

Schedule a poetry reading when the students can read selected poems. Encourage the poetry readers to practice the poems, heightening their effects with appropriate voice variations and inflections.

FANCIFUL HALLOWEEN

Two delightful picture book tales to share with younger readers are *A Woggle of Witches,* written and illustrated by Adrienne Adams; and *The Halloween Party* by Lonzo Anderson, illustrated by Adrienne Adams. *A Woggle . . .* tells of the activities of a group of witches on Halloween night as they go about their business of dining on bat stew and, of course, riding brooms. *The Halloween Party* features a young boy, Faraday Folsom, who stumbles on a witches' party and almost becomes a prime ingredient in their stew. Both volumes are gloriously illustrated in full color.

All ages will enjoy *Squeals, Squiggles and Ghostly Giggles* by Ann McGovern, a madcap treasury of stories, games poetry, tricks, and a skit designed for children to read, try out, and enjoy. Some of the activities might be included in your Halloween classroom celebration. Illustrations are by Jeffrey Higginbottom.

Three anthologies make up "The Albert Whitman Creatures Series" edited by Lee Bennett Hopkins. They include *A-Haunting We Will Go, Witching Time,* and *Monsters, Ghoulies and Creepy Creatures.* Each of the 128-page volumes include classic and contemporary stories, folktales from around the world, and verse by a wide range of authors such as Ruth-Manning Sanders, Sorche Nic Leodhas, Natalie Babbitt, and John Gardner. The books are illustrated in black-and-white drawings by Vera Rosenberry.

Just-right-reading for any day in October is *Jack-O'-Lantern* by Edna Barth, spiritfully relating how the first jack-o'-lantern evolved from the experiences of mean Jack and his encounter with the Devil. Attractive pictures are by Paul Galdone.

AMERICANA SCARES

American history is replete with its own assortment of ghost tales. Middle-graders might specialize for a time in these tales, beginning with three collections by Bruce and Nancy Roberts —*America's Most Haunted Places,* 15 stories about ghosts who haunt historic sites all over the United States; *Ghosts and Specters,* 10 American tales describing ghostly apparitions and happenings in the Deep South; and *Ghosts of the Wild West.* Excellent black-and-white photographs by the authors are as haunting as the tales.

Osceolo's Head and other American Ghost Stories by Walter Harter tells of such famous ghosts as John Wilkes Booth, Lincoln's assassin who haunts the Ford Theatre in Washington, D.C.; and Osceolo, the Seminole Indian chief who was jailed by American forces in the 1800s and later killed. The short tales are illustrated by Neil Waldman.

Creepy and mystifying folktales from diaries, documents, town records, and old collections of American folklore and re-told with wit and charm in *Tales Our Settlers Told* and *Ghost and Witches Aplenty: More Tales Our Settlers Told,* both by Joseph and Edith Raskin. Each volume includes 13 tales illustrated in black-and-white drawings by William Sauts Block.

After reading such tales, students might air views about whether or not they believe in ghosts and witches and then poll students in other classes for their opinions. Students might also try writing their own bewitching tales to compile into a class anthology.

As an alternative for children of all ages, suggest they draw and/or design individual haunted houses either in one-dimensional art forms or as dioramas or paper sculptures. After the projects are completed, review the use of adjectives by encouraging students to prepare a list that describes the finished products. Suggest that they make separate lists of scary words, loud words, quiet words, ghost and witchy words, adding them to pages in notebooks and referring to them throughout the year for other writing projects.

MYSTERY OF MYSTERIES

Introduce boys and girls to mystery books by devising a mini-mystery for the class via a book search. Hide several books somewhere in the room. Then write an announcement on the chalkboard telling students, "There's a mystery hiding in this room!" Oral or written clues can be given as to where the books might be found. Later the students who locate the books can each choose one to read. Suggest they tell about or read aloud one passage of their books to the rest of the class. For lower grades, a series of footprints cut from construction paper and taped on the floor can lead students to a mystery reading corner. Or place footprints on a bulletin-board display near a table featuring favorite scary titles.

Fine mysteries abound for readers of all ages. Old favorites for the younger set include four titles by Crosby Bonsall in Harper & Row's "I Can Read" mystery series. Titles are *The Case of the Cat's Meow, The Case of the Dumb Bells, The Case of the Scaredy Cats,* and *The Case of the Hungry Stranger,* which is also available in a Spanish-language edition, *El Caso del Forastero Hambriento,* translated by Pura Belpré. These delightful 64-page mysteries are illustrated in color by the author.

Another series for beginning readers are four titles by Elizabeth Levy—*Something Queer at the Ball Park, Something Queer at the Library, Something Queer is Going On,* and *Something Queer on Vacation.* These romps feature two super-sleuth girls, Gwen and Jill, lovable, contemporary kid-characters. Each of the 48-page volumes is illustrated in two-colors by Mordicai Gerstein.

Middle graders will enjoy knowing that an annual award, started in 1961, The Edgar Allen Poe Award, is given each spring by the Mystery Writers of America to honor the best juvenile mystery of the previous year. The award, a ceramic bust of Poe, is known as the "Edgar." For additional information on the award and a listing of winning authors and titles, write to the association at 105 East 19th Street, New York, New York 10003. After shivering through their readings, encourage students to select favorite books of this genre and create an award of their own. Books can be read, reread, and discussed, nominating three to five top choices and finally narrowing down the list to the best of the mystery crop.

You can hook girls and boys with this area of literature on Halloween and can keep it going throughout the school year to truly interest children in a wide variety of books.

REFERENCES[1]

Adams, Adrienne. *A Woggle of Witches.* Scribner, 1971; also available in paperback.

Anderson, Lonzo. *The Halloween Party.* Scribner, 1974; also available in paperback.

Barth, Edna. *Jack-O'-Lantern.* Seabury, 1974.

———. *Witches, Pumpkins and Grinning Ghosts: The Story of Halloween Symbols.* Seabury, 1972.

Borten. Helen. *Halloween.* Crowell, 1965.

Bonsall, Crosby. *The Case of the Cat's Meow.* Harper & Row, 1965.

———. *The Case of the Dumb Bells.* Harper & Row, 1966.

———. *The Case of the Hungry Stranger.* Harper & Row, 1963.

———. *The Case of the Scaredy Cats.* Harper & Row, 1971.

———, translated by Pura Belpre. *El Caso del Forastero Hambriento.* Harper & Row, 1969.

Harter, Walter. *Osceolo's Head and Other American Ghost Stories.* Prentice-Hall, 1974.

Hopkins, Lee Bennett. *A-Haunting We Will Go.* Whitman, 1977; Xerox paperback.

———. *Hey-How for Halloween.* Harcourt, 1974.

———. *Monsters, Ghoulies and Creepy Creatures.* Whitman, 1977.

———. *Witching Time.* Whitman, 1977.

Levy, Elizabeth. *Something Queer at the Ball Park.* Delacorte, 1975; also available in paperback.

———. *Something Queer at the Library.* Delacorte, 1977; also available in paperback.

———. *Something Queer is Going On.* Delacorte, 1973; also available in paperback.

———. *Something Queer on Vacation.* Delacorte, 1979.

McGovern, Ann. *Squeals, Squiggles and Ghostly Giggles.* Four Winds, 1973.

Patterson, Lillie. *Halloween.* Garrard, 1963.

Prelutsky, Jack. *It's Halloween.* Greenwillow, 1977.

Raskin, Joseph, and Edith Raskin. *Ghosts and Witches Aplenty: More Tales Our Settlers Told.* Lothrop, 1973.

[1]See Appendix for publishers' complete addresses.

————. *Tales Our Settlers Told.* Lothrop, 1971.
Roberts, Bruce, and nancy Roberts. *America's Most Haunted Places.* Doubleday, 1976.
————. *Ghosts and Specters.* Doubleday, 1974.
————. *Ghosts of the Wild West.* Doubleday, 1976.
Wallace, Daisy. *Witch Poems.* Holiday House, 1976.

20

Summertime and the reading is easy

Warm temperatures and the inviting outdoors pipe a message that children find hard to resist. To capitalize on their feelings of vacation-time anticipation, help them plan summertime reading lists that emphasize fun and learning.

Prevacation days are good times to review local public library hours and special summer programs. If possible, invite a local public librarian to visit your class or arrange for a visit to the library. This will acquaint children with specific upcoming events and answer their questions about library services offered during the summer months. The few but important minutes this will take to plan will provide boys and girls with hours, days, and nights of reading pleasure.

After the visit, have the class compile an annotated listing of favorite books they would recommend to others for summer reading. Suggest that they group the titles by genre—for example, novels (mysteries, humorous books, family stories, and so on), biographies, poetry, and nonfiction. Ask a parent or teacher-aide to type a stencil and mimeograph the list so that each child in the class will have a guide to good reading when they visit libraries.

You might also plan a summer book campaign by having students "advertise" their favorite book choices. Begin by introducing some of the basic techniques used in advertising campaigns. As early as 1938, the Institute for Propaganda Analysis identified such techniques including:

1. "Glad names"—particular words associated with pleasant feelings.
2. Transfer—the buyer of a product transfers his or her feelings to it.
3. Testimonial—well-known persons endorse a product.
4. Stacking the Cards—telling only a part of the truth.
5. Bandwagon approach—"everybody's doing it."

After discussing each of the categories with the class, ask them if they can think of popular advertisements that fit into each group. After they are familiar with advertising techniques, have them create book ads on large oaktag charts to advertise their personal choices for summer "must" reading. These can be displayed around the classroom, in the school library, or on hallway bulletin boards, along with a table display of the actual books being touted. Hold a "sell session" whereby students give their own sales pitches, encouraging others to read their selections.

The following books might be just right for several or all of your students to take along on a summer outing, to camp, to the seashore, or just to know about when all they want to do is lean against a tree trunk and read. Boys and girls can backpack a book as easily as a bathing suit, bat and ball, or transistor radio.

BOOKS TO TAKE TO WATER SITES

Thoughts of hot summer days often include water scenes of all kinds—from an icy lake to the lacy spray of a lawn sprinkler, from poolside to the ocean.

Down to the Beach by May Garelick is full of lyrical prose and beautiful watercolor paintings by Caldecott Award-winning artist Barbara Cooney. Young readers will discover boats and birds, shells and sand, and people and pebbles in this just-right book for beachgoers—or stay-at-homes. As a follow-up, students might write stories or minibooks about their own experiences at water sites. Or suggest they author a fantasy experience that they'd like to happen this coming summer. Students could also set up a display table of some of the beach objects mentioned in the book.

The titles listed below will allow older students to revel in the wonders of pond and stream life and enjoy a number of related activities.

In Ponds and Streams, written and illustrated by Margaret Waring Buck, is based on the author's observations and research. Although the volume focuses on the northeastern United States, it could also apply to many other parts of the country and southern Canada. This guide will help girls and boys identify and learn about different forms of nature such as underwater plants, flowers, insects and fish. *Pond Life* by George K. Reid is a more thorough guide to common plants and animals native to North American ponds and lakes. The book is packed with information, illustrations, and activities for young naturalists.

Other titles to look for include *Pond Life: Watching Animals Find Food,* and *Pond Life: Watching an Animal Grow Up* by Herbert H. Wong and Matthew F. Vessel.

BOOKS FOR ROUGHING-IT

Lewis and Clark, Admiral Byrd, and many children all have one outdoor activity in common—camping. For young children who may not have set up their first pup tent yet, try *Smokey Bear's Camping Book* by Irwin Shapiro. During an overnight hike, Smokey shows two children such things as how to choose equipment, pick a campsite, and pitch a tent. First-aid hints and water safety rules are also included. Bright, information-packed pictures by Mel Crawford illustrate each camping hint.

Going to Camp by Irene Cummings Kleeburg provides children with an introduction to camp life. The author discusses schedules, staffs, and what to bring to camp, as well as some of the anxieties one may feel when leaving home for an extended stay. A listing of four resources as to where children can get additional information is given. A glossary and index are appended. Black-and-white line drawings are by Tom Huffman.

Camping often provides do-it-yourselfers and outdoor chefs with an outlet for their talents. *For Campers Only: Sewing and Cooking* by Cameron and Margaret Yerian gives instructions on how to sew such items as backpacks, duffle bags, and belt pouches, and directions for cooking a variety of outdoor meals, from "bread twisters" to "corn on the coals."

For children who like to read first-person accounts, a small but attractive choice is *Five Days of Living with the Land* by Sarah Brown, illustrated with black-and-white line drawings by Bill Shields. In her "Foreword," the 15-year-old author describes herself as a "nature nut" who has devoured many books about survival in the woods, living off the land, and the idealism of it all. The text consists of her experiences in an uninhabited wooded area in Massachusetts for five summer days and four "long" nights, accompanied only by a Great Dane and a few bare essentials. Appended are lists of her necessities and seven books for information and enjoyment that she used before her "survival week."

Safety is emphasized in all the titles mentioned, but it is a good idea to caution children to be extra careful while engaging in any outdoor activity, with or without adult supervision. Consider extending invitations to a school nurse, local doctor, camp counselor, or an expert bike owner to discuss accident prevention and first-aid techniques.

BOOKS TO PLAY A PART IN

Producing a play, whether at a campsite, on a stoop, or in a park, is a good way for children to share summer hours in a creative and enjoyable way.

Small Plays for You and a Friend by Sue Alexander contains five short plays designed for two characters that will delight younger stars. Each is written skeletally so that children can "add" to the play, using their own imagination and creativity. The simplified format shows dialogue in color type; stage directions are printed in black. Illustrations are by Olivia H. H. Cole. Encourage each group of performers to add to their productions by including simple sound effects, using costumes, or even handing out programs. You might bring or ask students to bring in programs from shows, sports events, and so on. Discuss why programs are helpful and what kind of information they offer.

Middle graders who have been reared on the popular "Paddington" bear series created by Michael Bond will welcome *Paddington on Stage: Plays for Children* by Bond and Alfred Bradley. The collection features seven short plays and includes hints for props, sets, and costumes.

Older thespians will enjoy *The Tiger's Bones and Other Plays for Children*, a collection of five plays by the distinguished poet Ted Hughes. Included are "The Tiger's Bones," a fable about a curious type of scientist; "Beauty and the Beast," a variant of the folktale; and "Orpheus," based on the Greek myth.

Another source to look at is *Plays: The Drama Magazine for*

Young People, published monthly from October through May. This popular magazine is available at most public libraries or by subscription, $12.00 per year from Plays, Inc.

BOOKS TO TAKE PART IN

Tales of adventure and mystery are always welcome additions to any reading list for summer, when time abounds for children to sit and ponder plots, characters, and clues.

Encyclopedia Brown fans will hail the news that the world's foremost boy detective series by Don Sobel is now available in paperback editions from Bantam. In each book, Sobel cleverly gives solutions to a variety of mysteries solved by Leroy "Encyclopedia" Brown in a special section challenging readers to match wits with the 10-year-old mastermind of Idaville's war on crime. After reading books in this series, students might be inspired to try out their mystery writing skills. Or you might conceive a mystery. Divide students into detective squads and let each squad use its judgment to solve the mystery.

The Careless Animal by Ada and Frank Graham, Jr., presents nine ecological detective stories that describe how the actions of human beings have often had disturbing effects on the world. These short, easy-to-read, nonfiction accounts are set in various places in the world. The stories stimulate thinking about the interdependence of everything in nature and how a careless animal—in this case, a human—can disrupt nature's delicate balance.

Mature readers who want a challenge for summer reading might read *The Westing Game*, the 1979 Newbery Award-winning book written by Ellen Raskin.

A BOOK TO PICK A POEM FROM

Anytime is poetry time, but summer offers children many more moments to linger with a poem or even write one.

Near the Window Tree, written and illustrated by Karla Kuskin, is a joy for all ages and for all seasons. The book is a collection of 32 images, plus short paragraphs preceding each verse that tell how and why the author was inspired to write her poems. The poet plants wonder-ideas here and there, making *Near the Window Tree* the kind of book that sets summer minds to wondering and dreaming. Kuskin was the third recipient of the National Council of Teacher's of English Excellence in Poetry Award, 1979.

BOOKS TO READ BEFORE WHEELING

Summertime always suggests the use of wheels to get girls and boys from one place to another. Skateboarding and bicycling are two popular modes of transportation for both city and suburban children. Introducing them to books about the sports can serve to strengthen their skills as well as caution them on safety procedures they should know about.

Skateboarding is one childhood diversion that has become a nationwide sport. Skateboards come in a variety of shapes and sizes, from two-by-fours with skate wheels to well-engineered fiberglass, wood, or aluminum planks with specially constructed wheels. According to the Consumer Product Safety Commission, however, 28 persons have died in skateboard accidents since 1975; accidents requiring hospital treatment number more than 100,000 per year.

For advice on safe riding tips, how to select or build the right board, competition hints, and even a bit of board history, students can consult *Better Skateboarding for Boys and Girls* by Ross R. Olney and Chan Bush. Black-and-white photographs complete the volume. Mature readers will find out all they need to know in the *Skateboarder's Bible: Techniques, Equipment Stunts, Terms, Etc.* by Albert Cassorla. The appendices, worth the price of the book alone, include a bibliography and lists of associations, manufacturers, distributors, accessory makers, media, and skate parks, and a glossary.

A variety of books on bicycling can help children get a great deal of mileage from their treasured vehicles. One volume that will appeal to the average as well as above-average reader is *A Great Bicycle Book* by Jane Sarnoff, illustrated by Reynold Ruffins. And great it is! With clear, simple text and lively full-color pictures, the books shows that it is possible for children eight years old and up to maintain, repair, ride, race, and understand a bicycle. Sensible information is shared in a brief but important section on riding in the rain, on leaves, uphill, in the dark, and alongside a running, barking dog.

Also steer cyclists toward *Bike Ways: 101 Things You Can Do with a Bike* by Lillian and Godfrey Frankel, which explains how to organize a bike club, trips, tours, and campouts. Tips are given on riding—from beginner to racing—and on care, repair, and even bike photography. The text, illustrated with photographs, includes an index. Two additional titles which are up-to-date on bicycling activities are *Bicycling* by Charles Ira Coombs and *Better Bicycling for Boys and Girls* by George Sullivan.

GETTING AWAY FROM IT ALL AT HOME

Although many of your students may have travel plans, most will be spending at least some of their time at home. A backyard or nearby playground can be an ideal setting for summer adventures. Encourage the children to think of as many activities as they can, such as pet shows, talent revues, and garage plays, and hunt for complementary book titles. These ideas can be typed and duplicated as an informal "recreation schedule" for each child. Here are some suggestions to alleviate the "nothin' to do" doldrums.

Children sometimes need places where they can escape to be all by themselves. *Handmade Secret Hiding Places,* written and illustrated by Caldecott Award-winning Nonny Hogrogian, shows youngsters how to build 10 different inexpensive hideouts, from a cardboard-box house made from a mover's carton to a string hideaway that can be constructed wherever there is a group of trees. The book's ending note—"How many other hiding places can you make or find?"—may inspire children to put together their own volume of secret but safe hideaways.

Several children can collaborate on organizing a backyard art gallery. Paintings can be displayed by pinning them on a clothesline or a rope stretched between two poles or trees. Crafts items and models can be positioned on overturned boxes or picnic benches.

A neighborhood flea market or auction can provide days of fun and planning. Searching through closets, attics, and garages, and buying, bartering, and selling appeal to almost any child. And don't forget that it pays to advertise with homemade posters.

Turn the fruits and vegetables of summer into a mini-agribusiness with a community vegetable stand. *Vegetables in Patches and Pots: A Child's Guide to Organic Vegetable Growing* by Lorelie Miller Mintz shows how anyone, anywhere, can reap, sow, and harvest vegetables—from artichokes to water-

melons—in planters, pots, or boxes, along walls or fences, on
window ledges or fire escapes, or in a tiny corner patch of land.

REFERENCES[1]

Alexander, Sue. *Small Plays for You and a Friend.* Seabury, 1974;
    Scholastic paperback.
Bond, Michael, and Alfred Bradley. *Paddington on Stage: Plays for
    Children.* Houghton Mifflin, 1977.
Brown, Sarah. *Five Days of Living with the Land.* Addison-Wesley,
    1971.
Buck, Margaret Waring. *In Ponds and Streams.* Abingdon, 1953.
Cassorla, Albert. *Skateboarder's Bible: Techniques, Equipment,
    Stunts, Terms, Etc.* Running Press, 1977.
Coombs, Charles Ira. *Bicycling.* Morrow, 1972.
Frankel, Lillan, and Godfrey Frankel. *Bike Ways: 101 Things You Can
    Do with a Bike.* Sterling, 1972.
Garelick, May. *Down to the Beach.* Four Winds, 1973.
Graham, Ada, and Frank Graham, Jr. *The Careless Animal.* Double-
    day, 1975.
Hogrogian, Nonny. *Handmade Secret Hiding Places.* Viking, 1975.
Hughes, Ted. *The Tiger's Bones and Other Plays for Children.* Viking,
    1974.
Kleeburg, Irene Cummings. *Going to Camp.* Watts, 1978.
Kuskin, Karla. *Near the Window Tree.* Harper & Row, 1975.
Mintz, Lorelie Miller. *Vegetables in Patches and Pots: A Child's Guide
    to Organic Vegetable Gardening.* Farrar, Straus, 1976.
Olney, Ross R., and Charles Bush. *Better Skateboarding for Boys and
    Girls.* Dodd, Mead, 1977.
Raskin, Ellen. *The Westing Game.* Dutton, 1978.
Reid, George K. *Pond Life.* Golden, 1967; also available in paperback.
Sarnoff, Jane. *A Great Bicycle Book,* rev. ed. Scribner, 1973; also avail-
    able in paperback.
Shapiro, Irwin. *Smokey Bear's Camping Book.* Western, 1977.
Sobel, Don. *Encyclopedia Brown.* Thomas Nelson; Bantam paper-
    backs.
Sullivan, George. *Better Bicycling for Boys and Girls.* Dodd, Mead,
    1974.
Wong, Herbert H. *Pond Life: Watching an Animal Grow Up.* Addison-
    Wesley, 1970.
———. *Pond Life: Watching Animals Find Food.* Addison-Wesley,
    1970.
Yerian, Cameron, and Margaret Yerian. *For Camper's Only: Sewing
    and Cooking.* Children's Press, 1977.

[1]See Appendix for publishers' complete addresses.

PART V

Getting Involved

Book looking | Book making

Creating books of their very own—taking a manuscript from the idea stage, through to the writing and illustrating, and finally the finished bound product—will reinvest books with a unique value for children. Initiate a book-making project by first asking students to scrutinize their favorite volumes. Encourage them to pay close attention to every facet of a book, including dust jackets, bindings, endpapers, the title and dedication pages, and the graphics.

Set up a book-looking display table or shelf with a rich and wide variety of books. Include the artwork of Caldecott Award winners, as well as an assortment of other illustrators' techniques: collage designs of Leo Lionni; woodcuts by Ann Grifalconi; photography by Tana Hoban; and a multitude of black-and-white and full-color paintings by such artists as Anita and Arnold Lobel, Tom Feelings, Mercer Mayer, and Tomie de Paola.

After a sufficient period of looking, suggest that the children begin making their own books. They will need to decide whether to work individually or team up with a coauthor and/or illustrator. Several children might wish to go outside the classroom, inviting older siblings, parents, and grandparents to lend a hand at illustrating their work.

BOOKS ABOUT BOOK MAKING

Children who are eager to make their own books from scratch can consult *How To Make Your Own Books* by Harvey Weiss. The first section gives step-by-step instructions on how to make a book—from choosing paper, cutting and folding, binding and glueing to make covers, and deciding what kind of writing or printing to use. The second section presents a variety of book formats such as comic books, diaries, scrolls, books of rubbings, and nonsense sayings. The volume is illustrated with photographs and drawings.

Books: From Writer to Reader by Howard Greenfeld presents a different approach to learning about books and the publishing industry. This most comprehensive and lucid account of how books are produced relates how a book is born, beginning with an author's idea through to the finished volume. Readers will truly enjoy this inside guided tour of publishing. Numerous photographs and drawings are included as well as a glossary, bibliography, and index.

GETTING STARTED

You will probably find that some students will immediately plunge into writing their own original stories. Others, however, might need an idea or two to get them started. For these students, you might suggest an easy-to-execute ABC book. Have the children peruse a selection of these books to spark ideas of their own.

Two different, unique, and magnificently designed ABC collections are *Anno's Alphabet: An Adventure in Imagination* by Mitsumasa Anno, and *The Peaceable Kingdom: The Shaker Abecedarius*, illustrated by Alice and Martin Provenson. *Anno's Alphabet* features *trompe l'oeil* paintings that mystify the eyes and border designs that abound with curious curiosities. *The Peaceable Kingdom* offers the 26-line rhyme from "The Shaker Manifesto, 1882," which the Shakers used to teach children the alphabet. In addition to the big words, rhyme, and nonsense contained in this incongruous menagerie of animals, which all children will love, the Provensons give readers of all ages a distinguished volume featuring full-color paintings. An "Afterword" by Richard Meran Bersam contains information on Shaker history and education.

Older girls and boys will enjoy two books by Isaac Asimov: *ABC's of Space* and *ABC's of the Ocean*. In these volumes, A is for aquanaut, Q is for quaser, and Z is for zoogene. Blank spaces are provided under each letter, so that the children can collect and record new words. Both volumes are illustrated with photographs. Ideas I have seen come forth after children have looked carefully at a selection of ABC books are *The ABC's of Baseball*, *The ABC's of Television Shows*, and even *The ABC's of Karate*.

The alphabet technique has proved quite successful for many teachers across the country. One third-grade teacher in Fair Lawn, New Jersey, uses the approach to culminate various units, having the class prepare a complete book from start to finish. Students work together in groups writing and illustrating their books on 8 1/2-X-11" paper. When this is completed, they recreate their work on stencils, and a cover is designed by a class artist. When the stencils are run off and collated, the children bind them by stitching the edges with colored yarn. Copies of the completed books are given to each child to take home, and a copy is placed in the school library. A completed project is an alphabet book—*The ABC's of Fall*—to culminate a unit on nature at a nearby pond. The class had visited the pond to study nature *au naturel*! The class was alive with pond flora and fauna, nonfiction trade books, stories, poems, filmstrips, and busy child-authors.

POETRY PEG

If children have been exposed to a variety of poetry and poets, they could compile minianthologies of favorite verses, selecting poems dealing with a specific theme. A trip to any library will acquaint students with a numerous amount of theme anthologies on any grade or interest level.

To give students the idea behind specific books of this kind, steer them toward such diverse collections as *An Arkful of Animals: Poems for the Very Young,* selected by William Cole, with black-and-white drawings by Lynn Munsinger; and *Go to Bed: A Book of Bedtime Poems,* selected by Lee Bennett Hopkins, with black-and-white illustrations by Rosekrans Hoffman. Cole's volume features a wide range of poets, from Conrad Aiken to Valerie Worth, paying tribute to real and imaginary feathered, furry, and flying animals children are familiar with.

Hopkins' collection contains 20 poems depicting the pleasant and sometimes unpleasant aspects of bedtime.

Middle graders will be charmed by *Amelia Mixed the Mustard and Other Poems*, 20 poems about girls selected and illustrated by Caldecott Award-winning artist Evaline Ness. Rebellious Abigail, greedy Jane, eat-it-all Elaine—girls of all sizes, shapes, dispositions, and desires are featured in this joyous collection.

Older readers can glean ideas from two anthologies compiled by Nancy Larrick, *Room for Me and a Mountain Lion: Poetry of Open Space* and *On City Streets*, rich compilations of poetry selected with the help of student poetry readers and lovers.

Encourage children to tuck in original poems in their minianthologies, also,—either verse written by them or by classroom peers. Sister Marietta from Wichita, Kansas, has her sixth graders prepare and illustrate their own minipoetry booklets. After children select a favorite poem, they set out to design and illustrate booklets. A cover is designed; a title page lists the poet and illustrator. After the pages are stapled, students delight as they become anthologists.

Primary graders might design poetry shape books by cutting out basic shapes (squares, circles, triangles, rectangles) or the shape of a person or animal character from construction paper. The shape alone might dictate what the theme of the anthology will be about. One first-grade class created an anthology called "Round Poems," dealing with objects such as wheels, oranges, and other circular objects. After a batch of circles were cut out to form the book's inside pages, children wrote and illustrated definitions of a circle opening with, "A circle is round and round. It can never stop because no one knows where it started." Cut-out circles made from colored oaktag were used for the book's covers. Copied-down poems made up the bulk of the anthology. On the last page, they wrote a few lines "about the author," and attached snapshots of themselves.

SHARING FINISHED PROJECTS

Young authors will want to share their finished books. This desire can be satisfied in a variety of ways. Finished volumes can be given as family gifts for holidays or birthdays. They might also be donated to the school or public library for others to read. One school librarian in Maine includes data on student-made books in the card catalogue.

Third-grade students in North Carolina displayed their creations at a spring festival. Their teacher reported that a higher incentive for reading developed after her students were involved in book-making projects.

Older students might write and illustrate stories for children in the lower grades. This is a particularly good project to launch with groups of children who are having difficulties in reading and writing skills.

Ideas such as these provide rich rewards for all our junior authors.

REFERENCES[1]

Anno, Mitsumasa. *Anno's Alphabet: An Adventure in Imagination*. Crowell, 1975.

Asimov, Isaac. *ABC's of Space*. Walker, 1970.

———. *ABC's of the Ocean*. Walker, 1970.

Cole, William, ed. *An Arkful of Animals: Poems for Young Readers*. Houghton Mifflin, 1978.

Greenfeld, Howard. *Books: From Writer to Reader*. Crown, 1976; also available in paperback.

Hopkins, Lee Bennett, selector. *Go to Bed!: A Book of Bedtime Poems*. Knopf, 1979.

Larrick, Nancy, ed. *On City Streets*. Evans, 1968; Bantam paperback.

———. *Room for Me and A Mountain Lion: Poetry of Open Space*. Evans, 1974.

Ness, Evaline, ed. *Amelia Mixed the Mustard and Other Poems*. Scribner, 1975.

Provenson, Alice, and Martin Provenson. *The Peaceable Kingdom: The Shaker Abecedarius*. Viking, 1978.

Weiss, Harvey. *How To Make Your Own Books*. Crowell, 1974.

[1]See Appendix for publishers' complete addresses.

Cooking with children's literature

"Some books are to be tasted, others to be swallowed, and some few to be chewed and digested," said Sir Francis Bacon. While he was referring to the appeal and value of different kinds of volumes, there are titles that do provide literal and real nourishment—cookbooks. When these are based on or complemented by well-loved children's stories, the combination is unbeatable for developing a variety of tastes and skills.

PRIMARY PIÈCE DE RÉSISTANCE

A cooking center for primary-grade children is an excellent setting in which to practice following directions, doing math, and developing motor abilities by pouring liquids, kneading dough, and cracking eggs. With an array of utensils, ingredients, and charts on safety and health tips, youngsters are ready for their first pièce de résistance.

To launch culinary sessions, try the collection of recipes inspired by well-known tales and rhymes in *Pease Porridge Hot: A Mother Goose Cookbook,* written and illustrated by Lorinda Bryan Cauley. This includes recipes for such delights as "The Cow Jumped Over the Moon's Moooooo Shake!" "Hansel and Gretel's Healthy Children's Cookie House," and "The Little Old Woman's Catch-Me-If-You-Can Gingerbread Man." A front page lists "Tips to Remember Before Cooking," and a glossary is appended. The attractive format—a recipe and a full-page, black-and-white picture per double-page spread—has great appeal. The fact that *sesame* (as in seeds) in the illustration on page 15 is misspelled could inspire an "error-in-the-artwork" search. Consider awarding a small bottle or bag of the seeds to the winner to make "The Big Bad Wolf's Little Pigs in a Blanket (Enough for Four Famished Wolves)"—or humans!

"Pooh" fans will love the idea of that silly old bear's mixing things up in *The Pooh Cook Book* by Virginia H. Ellison, inspired by the works of A. A. Milne with illustrations by Ernest H. Shepard. This collection features over 60 recipes, each with an appropriate quotation from the "Pooh" series. In a short Introduction, the author offers some sound reading advice: "If you've never read these books, why not start at the beginning of *Winnie-the-Pooh* and read the 10 chapters in it, one at each meal, and then the 10 in *The House at Pooh Corner*? Then, when you use *The Pooh Cook Book* you can play a game of 'Guessing-Which-Chapter-the-Quotation-Comes-From.' "

Among the seven sections are "Breakfasts," "Smackerels, Elevenses and Teas," "Christmas Specialties," and, of course, "Honey Sauces." An index of recipes is appended.

RABBIT FOOD

Beautifully illustrated with Beatrix Potter's original black-and-white and full-color illustrations is *Peter Rabbit's Natural Foods Cookbook* by Arnold Dobrin. Featured are beloved characters who "share" such goodies as "Alder Rat Squeaker's Homemade Peanut Butter," "Mr. McGregor's Scrumptious Puréed Beets," and "Peter and Benjamin's Super Tossed Salad." Dobrin states in his preface: "If you eat nourishing foods, and do not overeat, I doubt that you will ever have to be put to bed, as was poor Peter, with a cup of hot chamomile tea." This fitting quotation might be just right for a bulletin board display of foods for healthy eating. The last chapter gives helpful hints on cooking, boiling and stir-frying vegetables, cooking an egg, and chopping. Included are an index and a complete listing of illustration sources.

All of the above titles could be used to encourage youngsters to hunt for foods mentioned in other stories and to find related recipes. Hand-drawn pictures of the characters to accompany carefully handwritten recipes will result in handsome mini-cookbooks to take home as gifts for parents.

LITERARY CHEFS

The following three intriguing titles offer a slightly different approach to cooking with literature for middle-grade youngsters.

Storyteller Ellin Greene has compiled two handsome volumes—*Clever Cooks: A Concoction of Stories, Charms, Recipes and Riddles* and *Midsummer Magic: A Garland of Stories, Charms and Recipes.* The first title presents a baker's dozen of stories involving clever cooks who outwit fairies, giants, kings, and ordinary people. Interspersed among the tales are recipes and riddles. For example, following the story "The Old Woman Who Lost Her Dumpling" are directions for making "Cherry Dumplings." The volume is illustrated with black-and-white line drawings by Trina Schart Hyman. The same format is followed in *Midsummer Magic,* illustrated with black-and-white drawings by Barbara Cooney.

Mary Poppins devotees will find that her culinary abilities leave no room for doubt in *Mary Poppins in the Kitchen: A Cookery Book with a Story* by P. L. Travers, written in collaboration with culinary consultant Maurice Moore-Betty and illustrated by Mary Shephard, the original artist of the Poppins characters. As Mr. Banks, one of the inhabitants of the legendary house at Number Seventeen Cherry Tree Lane notes, "Mary Poppins can do everything!" The tale begins with the indomitable governess' teaching the Banks children how to prepare daily three-meal menus and how to observe safe kitchen procedures. Through it all, a parade of old friends—the Bird Woman, Admiral Boom, and more—drop in to help. The 75-plus recipes, arranged from A to Z (Angel Cake to Zodiac Cake), are easy enough for the child who has little kitchen experience, yet enticing enough for the accomplished boy or girl cook.

SAVORY, SONGFUL SOUP

Poetry and music seem to lend themselves very well to the delights of soup. Perhaps this is due to the rich imagery of simmering, stirring, and slurping. But whatever the reason may be, you will want to share these two popular soup songs with boys and girls of all ages.

The classic two-stanza paean to soup sung by the Mock Turtle in Chapter 10 of Lewis Carroll's *Alice's Adventures in Wonderland* is a gem:

Beautiful Soup, so rich and green,
Waiting in a hot tureen!
Who for such dainties would not stoop?
Soup of the evening, beautiful Soup!

      Beau-ootiful Soo——oop!
      Beau-ootiful Soo——oop!
      Soo——oop of the e——e——evening,
      Beautiful, beautiful Soup!

Beautiful Soup! Who cares for fish,
Game, or any other dish?
Who would not give all else for two pennyworth only of beautiful
Soup?

      Beau-ootiful Soo——oop!
      Beau-ootiful Soo——oop!
      Soo——oop of the e——e——evening,
      Beautiful, beauti-FUL SOUP!

Maurice Sendak's *Really Rosie Starring the Nutshell Kids,* based on the television program, contains the text to "Chicken Soup With Rice," along with the musical score written by Carole King.

Encourage students to hunt for other food songs or poems—from soup to nuts—or to write their own to share with others. These can be written on or attached to paper plates and arranged on a "What's Cooking?" bulletin board display, along with cups, napkins, and plastic utensils.

Another possibility is to hold a "multicourse" concert. Have small groups of children each sing or play food-related songs that make up an imaginary meal. For example, one group could start off with "Chicken Soup With Rice" and other food songs such as "Food, Glorious Food" from the Broadway musical and film, *Oliver.* The "desserts" could be "Shoo Fly Pie and Apple Pan Dowdy," "Life is Just a Bowl of Cherries," and "Yes, We Have No Bananas." For a nut-like encore try, "Eating Goober Peas."

For additional ideas, consult *Hot Cross Buns and Other Old Street Cries,* chosen by John Langstaff with pictures by Nancy Winslow Parker. Herein, such music and lyrics to such ditties as "Gingerbread," "Milk," "Strawberries," "Mutton Pies," "Walnuts," and of course, "Hot-Cross Buns," are featured.

Move over, Julia Child. Make room, Charles Beard. Here comes a whole new generation of cooks who know their books.

REFERENCES[1]

Carroll, Lewis. *Alice's Adventures in Wonderland.* Available in many hardbound and paperback editions.

Cauley, Lorinda Bryan. *Pease Porridge Hot: A Mother Goose Cookbook.* Putnam, 1977.

Dobrin, Arnold. *Peter Rabbit's Natural Foods Cookbook.* Warne, 1977.

Ellison, Virginia H. *The Pooh Cook Book.* Dutton, 1969; Dell paperback.

Greene, Ellin. *Clever Cooks: A Concoction of Stories, Charms, Recipes and Riddles.* Lothrop, 1973.

———. *Midsummer Magic: A Garland of Stories, Charms and Recipes.* Lothrop, 1976.

Langstaff, John. *Hot Cross Buns and Other Old Street Cries.* Atheneum, 1978.

Sendak, Maurice. *Really Rosie Starring the Nutshell Kids.* Harper & Row paperback, 1975.

Travers, P. L. *Mary Poppins in the Kitchen: A Cookery Book with a Story.* Harcourt, 1975; also available in paperback.

[1]See Appendix for publishers' complete addresses.

23

Help wanted!
Jobs for tomorrow

The United States Office of Education has established 15 career clusters that encompass almost all existing job roles: They include agribusiness and natural resources; business and office; communications and media; construction; consumer and homemaking-related occupations; environmental control; fine arts and humanities; health; hospitality and recreation; manufacturing; marine science; marketing and distribution; personal service; public service; transportation.

How do your children view work? What do they feel is the difference between a job and a career? What types of job roles are their parents engaged in? Such questions might provoke thinking about career awareness and also help you get an idea of what your students already know and what their attitudes are.

What jobs do the children do now in school? At home? Help students explore the idea that a job entails responsibility, conscientiousness, enjoyment. Then move into a broader consideration of careers by suggesting that the students discuss different job roles they might like. Why did they make these choices? Do they think their choices might change over the next few years? Discuss what each occupation entails.

Can the children match their job selection with the appropriate United States Office of Education cluster? The students' names and initial career choices could be compiled into an ongoing chart and kept on display. Other jobs encountered during the study could be added to the chart under the correct cluster. At the end of the unit, students could note whether their ideas, choices, or attitudes changed and, if so, why.

A LOOK AT JOBS

In the next phase of your career study, you might focus on particular jobs. *When You Grow Up,* a set of 15 13 x 20" posters, produced by Mini-Productions, Inc., features a stylized depiction of a child dressed in career gear. The teacher's guide on each poster's reverse side provides learning objectives, a brief read-aloud story about the job category, questions, and suggestions for projects in various curriculum areas. A listing of reference materials is also included. Complement the posters with *Supersuits* by Vicki Cobb, illustrated by Peter Lippman. Diagrams, poetry, and a multitude of exciting facts are presented about people who endure severe environmental conditions in their work and who require special clothing to survive. The book encourages boys and girls to dive into watery depths, sail into space, fight blazing flames, endure freezing weather, and immerse themselves in this superb text suited to middle-grade readers.

Try to arrange for guests from different fields to visit your class. Some could be parents, including mothers and fathers who work at home as homemakers or in other roles. Have the children prepare questions to ask upcoming guests. Information gathered from visitors can then be compiled into a directory of "Careers and People in Them" and used as an ongoing reference. Arrangements can also be made for students to make on-location visits to job sites—especially those students who show marked interest in a particular line of work.

I Found Them in the Yellow Pages by Norma Farber is a picture alphabet book that will inspire a host of projects. It features all kinds of job roles—from acrobats to zookeepers, printed on yellow pages, of course, with excellent illustrations by Marc Brown.

From their readings thus far, the children can assemble their own career dictionaries by pasting sheets of white paper onto the Yellow Pages from a discarded telephone directory. They should have 26 pages, one for each letter of the alphabet. On each page they can write job titles (corresponding to the alphabet letter of the page) and descriptions, and include illustrations or related magazine cutouts.

WOMEN AT WORK

Career awareness also offers opportunities to focus on the current drive for equal employment for women in today's society. Use *I Am!,* written and illustrated by Sonia O. Lisker, to spark primary graders to think about nonsexist occupations. The story is about an energetic girl who plays a fast and funny game of careers, becoming such things as a mail carrier, fire fighter, and milk deliverer.

Two other titles—*Mommies at Work* by Eve Merriam, illustrated by Caldecott Award-winning artist Beni Montresor; and *Mothers Can Do Anything,* written and illustrated by Joe Lasker—point out that, in addition to their homemaking role, many mothers can and do have full-time jobs. How many students' mother work outside the home? How do the children feel about this situation? Do the children consider homemaking a job? Why? Why not? Are any students' fathers househusbands?

Plan a bulletin board display that features drawings and/or actual photographs of mothers at work. As an accompanying project, a survey could be taken of how many of the students' mothers do work outside the home and how many girls in class plan to have careers.

The women's liberation movement has surely been an impetus for the "What Can She Be" series by Gloria and Esther Goldreich. These easy-to-read books for middle and upper graders include such titles as *What Can She Be? A Newscaster; ... An Architect; ... A Musician; ... A Lawyer; ... A Veterinarian; ... A Farmer;* and *... A Geologist.*[1] Each title, illustrated with black-and-white photographs, introduces the multifaced aspects of a career through descriptions of a woman involved in it.

I Can Be Anything: Careers and Colleges for Young Women by Joyce Slayton Mitchell, an excellent guide for mature readers presented in alphabetical order, cites over 100 careers for

[1]For a complete listing of titles in this and other series discussed herein, write to the publisher for a descriptive brochure or their complete catalog, marked: Attention: Juvenile Books.

women from accountant to zoologist. Each brief job description tells, "What It's Like to Be . . .," the education and skills needed, the future for women in the field, salaries, schools, universities and colleges, and addresses for further information. Black-and-white photographs of women at work are included.

Encourage middle graders to delve into fiction and biographies, too, to find examples of women at work. Discussions of fictional characters as well as real people can lead children to understand what women's liberation truly means.

OTHER CAREER AWARENESS SERIES

Each of the 15 titles in the "Community Helpers" series published by Albert Whitman and Company deals with a service or industry and features men and women of different races, ages, and backgrounds. Although designed for the lower grades, upper graders, particularly reluctant readers, will find the books useful. Each of the titles are 32 pages long and are illustrated.

Younger readers will also enjoy the series, "What Does A _____ Do?" published by Dodd, Mead, and Company. Careers covered include a guardsman, congressman, cowboy, VISTA volunteer, Secret Service agent, senator, veterinarian, and lifeguard. Black-and-white photographs are used to illustrate each volume.

Thirty-four "Early Career Books" are published by Lerner Publishing Company; they describe nearly 500 occupations in industry, civil service, sports, agriculture, community service, and the arts, each illustrated with full-color photographs on each double-page spread. In addition to the books, filmstrip sets, cassettes, teacher's guides, and study prints are also available.

Although the Lippincott "I-Like-To-Read-Books" series are not fact-filled regarding specific careers covered, they are a delight for the tinier-career minded youngster. Four books appear in this series: *I Am A Ballerina, I Am A Chef, I Am A Farmer,* and *I Am A Fisherman,* all written and illustrated by Dick Swayne and Peter Savage. Each book follows a youngster as they engage in pertinent job roles. The beauty of the books is their design with full-color, charming photographs gracing each page and a simple brief text set in large type.

Steer older readers toward "Exploring Careers," a series published by Lothrop that includes 15 titles coinciding with the previously mentioned United Stated Office of Education clusters. Each title covers the kinds of jobs available in a particular field, the type of work done, the skills and aptitudes needed, the training and eduction required, and the possibilities for advancement. Some list related book titles, as well as places where students can write for additional information. The "Vocations in Trade" series, also published by Lothrop, written by Arthur Liebers, is packed with photographs and information about people who work with their hands. The books provide practical advice about how students can prepare for the field and what opportunities are available in vocational schools, community colleges, and state apprenticeship programs.

A wealth of up-to-date material is also provided in the paperback series, "Adventures in the World of Work," published by Random House. Each book focuses on one field of work and features first-person accounts of 10 or more people working at different jobs in a particular field. They discuss duties, coworkers, and surroundings, the training or education their occupation requires, personal qualities that helped them succeed, and how their job fits into the entire industry. Included in each book are brief descriptions of up to 15 other jobs in the field and a list of sources for further information. Three of the titles in this series are: *Who Puts the Grooves in the Record?* by Alice Edmunds, *Who Puts the Plane in the Air?* by Dina Anastasio, and *Who Puts the Print on the Page?* by Howard Langer. The volumes are illustrated with black-and-white photographs.

You can help bring jobs for tomorrow into clearer focus for students of today by using and discussing available materials to develop understanding and awareness.

REFERENCES[2,3]

Cobb, Vicki, *Supersuits.* Lippincott, 1975; also available in paperback.
Farber, Norma. *I Found Them in the Yellow Pages.* Little, Brown, 1973; also available in paperback.
Lasker, Joe. *Mothers Can Do Anything.* Whitman, 1972.
Lisker, Sonia O. *I Am!* Hastings House, 1975.
Merriam, Eve. *Mommies at Work.* Scholastic paperback.
Mitchell, Joyce Slayton. *I Can Be Anything: Careers and Colleges for Young Women.* Bantam paperback.

[2]For titles other than those in series.
[3]See Appendix for publishers' complete addresses.

Smile! Say, "Cheese!"
Children as photographers

"Many people do not consider photography a project for five-year-olds ... (but) it makes sense to let children learn about photography as early as possible. It teaches them to look around and discuss their surroundings, to observe and tell with pictures more than they can describe with words." This excerpt from "Note to Adults" in Nina Leen's book *Taking Pictures* offers solid reasons for putting cameras in the hands of youngsters, whether they are 5 or 15. With easy-to-operate equipment, a few simple directions, and a good selection of books on photography, almost any child can capture on film his or her unique way of looking at the world.

AIM, CLICK, ADVANCE THE FILM

A good way to start a photography project for young children is with the simple vocabulary and black-and-white photographs in Leen's *Taking Pictures* and Robin Forbes' *Click! A First Camera Book*. Both authors present basic information about the camera, directions on how to shoot indoor and outdoor pictures, and some novel ideas on how even the youngest shutterbug can be creative with a camera.

To help children become adept at changing film, focusing, and centering pictures, invite a parent camera buff or someone from a local camera shop to discuss techniques and answer questions. If possible, follow up with a visit to a film processing plant so that girls and boys can see firsthand what happens to those precious rolls of film.

Once they are familiar with the mechanics of picture taking, ask students for ideas on how they can put their newfound skills to best use in the classroom. For example, in a project conducted in several schools in the Harlem area of New York City, both teachers and children used cameras to "catch" classmates in the process of learning. They took such shots as a child engrossed in reading, a group of students working together on an art project, and friends figuring out math problems on the chalkboard. A team who won a relay race, participants in a spelling bee competition, and high points of field trips were also recorded on film. Mounting the pictures in albums and occasionally displaying them provided the children with candid portrayals of how they looked and acted in different situations. Self-concepts soared as admirers complimented each photographer's work.

CRITICAL VIEWERS AND THINKERS

Classroom photography sessions can be related to almost any subject matter, but they can be especially effective in practicing thinking skills. Planning shots, sequencing photos to tell a story, and evaluating a picture's impact are just a few examples.

To further enhance these skills, take a sharp look with your students at two volumes by Patricia Ruben, *What Is New? What Is Missing? What Is Different?* and *True or False?* On each left-hand page of *What Is New?* ... there is a group of pictures which, at first glance, may look the same as those on the right-hand page. But when children carefully examine them, they will notice the new, the missing, or the different. In *True or False?* the photographs require viewers to make deductions based on the situations pictured. For example, the first picture shows two children happily holding hands. The text reads: "Holly Jo and Dana seem to be friends. Is this true or false?"

Another book to share with younger children is Tana Hoban's *Is It Red? Is It Yellow? Is It Blue?* This is Hoban's first full-color book of photography and it is masterful at every turn of the page. The photographs introduce colors and the concepts of shape, quantity, and direction.

A different approach to sharpen children's ability to make careful observations is offered in *Is This A Baby Dinosaur? and other Science Picture-Puzzles* by Millicent E. Selsam. Readers study black-and-white close-ups of things found in nature to guess what they really are before finding the answer on the following page. For example, a charming photograph of two puzzling-looking creatures asks, "Are these baby dinosaurs?" Flipping the page reveals they are actually baby pelicans.

ART AND HISTORY

The history and creativity of photography are fascinating subjects for older students to persue. One intriguing text on photography as a fine art is *The Art of Photography* by Shirley Glubok, designed by Gerald Nook. It surveys black-and-white pictures from the 1830s to the present, focusing on outstanding photographers and their work. Examples begin with the earliest daguerreotypes and calotypes (photographs reproduced from a paper negative), continuing to news shots, portraits, and landscapes. The beauty and vitality of these photographs are unforgettable.

Two volumes for middle-grade history and photography buffs alike are *Photographing History: The Career of Mathew Brady* by Dorothy and Thomas Hoobler and *The Story of American Photography: An Illustrated History for Young People* by Martin Sandler. The Hoobler book, a biography, is illustrated with Brady's photographs of various Civil War battle sites and soldier poses. These dramatically depict not only the spirit of an era, but also the genius of this master photographer. An index is appended. Sandler's history of American photography presents the works of such pioneers as Samuel Morse, George Eastman, and Mathew Brady. Clear and concise, this lavishly produced and designed volume contains over 200 pictures, many in full color, including a section of photographs commissioned by the Office of Economic Opportunity in the 1960s.

Such volumes can motivate children to hunt for old photographs in attics, cellars, and garages. In addition to conducting research on whom the pictures were taken of, children might also investigate who the photographers were and what the settings were, or discuss posing styles and the quality of the prints.

CAPTURING A COMMUNITY ON FILM

Community life can be a lively subject for photo stories of all kinds. For example, students might enjoy taking pictures of their houses or apartment buildings, playgrounds, favorite stores, and places of worship and putting them together to form an illustrated neighborhood map.

Recently, a group of fourth graders in Missouri snapped pictures of workers in their community—butchers, bakers, mail carriers, and store and school personnel—for a career awareness project. After developing and mounting the photographs, the students held a party to which they invited the subjects to see a gallery display of their efforts.

The inspiration for this idea came from two books of photographs the children had closely studied: *Women at Their Work* by Betty Lou English and *And What Do You Do? A Book About People and Their Work* by George Ancona. *Women ...* is a series of double-page spreads showing 21 women in a variety of jobs, including an airplane pilot, rabbi, dentist, and jockey. Each briefly discusses her occupation. *And What Do You Do?* introduces 21 men and women involved in careers that do not require a college degree. Among the occupations are a tugboat deckhand, mechanic, chef, and air traffic controller. The attractiveness of these books and their easy-to-read descriptions make them fine choices for children of all ages.

Since its invention in 1839 by Louis Daguerre, photography has become an important part of our lives. We can keep cameras clicking, children smiling and saying, "Cheese!" and recording now-moments forever with fine volumes such as the above as our guide.

REFERENCES[1]

Ancona, George. *And What Do You Do? A Book About People and Their Work.* Dutton, 1976.

English, Betty Lou. *Women at Their Work.* Dial, 1977.

Forbes, Robin. *Click! A First Camera Book.* Macmillan, 1979.

Glubok, Shirley. *The Art of Photography.* Macmillan, 1977.

Hoban, Tana. *Is It Red? Is It Yellow? Is It Blue?* Greenwillow, 1977.

Hoobler, Dorothy, and Thomas Hoobler. *Photographing History: The Career of Mathew Brady.* Putnam, 1977.

[1]See Appendix for publishers' complete addresses.

Leen, Nina. *Taking Pictures.* Holt, Rinehart and Winston, 1977.
Ruben, Patricia. *True or False? Lippincott, 1978; also available in paperback.*
———. *What Is New? What Is Missing: What Is Different?* Lippincott, 1978.
Sandler, Martin. *The Story of American Photography: An illustrated History for Young People.* Little, Brown, 1979.
Selsam, Millicent. *Is This A Baby Dinosaur? and other Science Picture-Puzzles.* Harper & Row, 1972; Scholastic paperback.

PART VI

More Than Just Fun

Ha-ha and voilà:
Books of humor and magic

When I arrived for a visit at a friend's third-grade class, she warned me, "You picked a gloomy day. Nothing seems to be working—including me! The kids are tuned out, terribly tired, and feeling the blahs."

I empathized with her, knowing well the feeling those kinds of days can bring.

"But," she continued, "when the blahs beat us down, I can always rely on a funny book. Watch how this revives the class."

Turning to the children, she said, "I think it's time for a story. I'm going to 'Amelia Bedelia' you for a while."

At once the dismal atmosphere turned to bursting enthusiasm. "Yippees," "yeahs," and "greats" filled the classroom as my friend began reading *Amelia Bedelia and the Surprise Shower* by Peggy Parish, illustrated by Fritz Siebel. Ms. Bedelia, of course, is the Roger family's eccentric maid who carries out her instructions to the letter.

By the time the teacher had gotten to page 15, the children were high on the humor. So was I! For at this point, when Amelia Bedelia is asked to prune the hedges, she goes to the cupboard for a box of prunes and proceeds to stick them all over the shrubs! Such plays-on-words are what the "Amelia Bedelia" books are all about. All of the titles in this wonderful series of books are effective with boys and girls on all grade levels.

A splash of humor and magic is always a welcome addition to classroom reading. You, too, can dispel the "dismals" by launching a look at humorous books. To begin, ask the children, "What is the funniest book you have ever read?" This simple question can yield many titles that the students can seek out, read, and share. As they discuss the characters and situations, ask for their opinions on what is humorous to them and why it is that some people laugh at things that others do not find funny at all. The wide variety of books dealing with humor and magic will not only entertain but also educate. They can serve to reinforce important language arts skills through reading, speaking, listening, and creative drama activities.

The "ha-ha" books featured herein are rich sources of fun and fact. The "voilàs" demand that girls and boys carefully read step-by-step directions or they will be quickly pooh-poohed by their audiences. A bonus of this genre is that such titles can be read, used, and enjoyed by even the most reluctant readers, because the selections are short and the vocabulary is accessible.

Introduce humor to the class by discussing the various kinds. Summarize this discussion by asking students to write a definition of humor. The children will soon realize that a sense of humor is a very personal thing.

Gather and display a variety of humorous books and materials. After the students have looked over and laughed at the titles, ask each child to choose a funny selection, a joke, or a trick that will astound and surprise. These can be rehearsed and performed in a "Joke and Magic Festival" for other classes or the entire school.

HA-HAS FOR SOCIAL STUDIES

Humorous books that deal with pure Americana offer a natural tie-in to social studies units.

Five titles by Alvin Schwartz contain a collection of material from children, adults, and folklore archives around the country. The titles are *A Twister of Twists, a Tangler of Tongues: Tongue Twisters*; *Tomfoolery: Trickery and Foolery with Words*; *Witcracks: Jokes and Jests from American Folklore*; *Cross Your Fingers, Spit in Your Hat: Superstitions and Other Beliefs*; *Whoopers: Tall Tales and Other Lies*. Each title includes "Notes and Sources" that older children can use to glean

valuable information. The total collection of titles, illustrated
by Glen Rounds, will expand their understanding of humor as
a part of American life and history. You might suggest that
students gather found bits of local folklore, tall tales, and so on,
and send them to Alvin Schwartz, who welcomes letters from
students and teachers. Correspondence can be sent to him in
care of the publisher, J. B. Lippincott.

Duncan Emrich's *The Nonsense Book of Tongue-Twisters,
Puzzles and Jokes from American Folklore, The Hodgepodge
Book*, and *The Whim-Wham Book* are also rich collections
culled from American folklore. These books, each illustrated
by Ib Ohlsson, are certain to spark some humorous collections
by the students themselves, either in individual or class booklets, containing favorite jokes, riddles, puns, tall tales, rhymes,
tongue twisters, or their own whim-whams. Encourage the
children to listen to families and friends for bits of humor to
include in their collections.

SCIENCE SNICKERS

Two paperback books from Scholastic Book Services can be
used to introduce younger readers to basic science concepts.
Science Riddles by Rose Wyler poses such riddles as "What is
a caterpillar after it is three days old?" Flipping the page we
find the answer—"Four days old"—along with an explanation
of how long it takes for a caterpillar to spin and come out of its
cocoon as a butterfly. *Prove It!* by Rose Wyler and Gerald Ames
cites fun-to-do science experiments using ordinary household
items.

The "Science for Fun" series by Laurence B. White, Jr., illustrated by Marc Tolon Brown, includes four titles: *Science Puzzles, Science Games, Science Toys,* and *Science Tricks.* The
books give a sound approach to simple science experiments
that are fun and easy to do, using readily available materials.
Young readers are enticed into experiments with air pressure,
gravity, sound, electricity, and other scientific concepts. Activities are presented in simple vocabulary and include directions
for making a raisin dance, growing a mold garden, seeing water in a potato, and cleaning a dirty penny with chemicals. You
can use these experiments to teach basic concepts and they will
add some magic and fun to science study on all grade levels.

Madcap science funnies are included in the chapter, "The

Science Scene," in *Jokes, Puns and Riddles* by David Allen Clark. One of the just-for-laughs tidbits is:

Don: Do you know what would happen if you swallowed uranium?
Ron: Nope.
Don: You'd get a-tomic ache.

And there are 288 pages of more jests like this. Black-and-white line drawings are by Leonard Kalish.

HUMOR IN POETRY

Verse is a good medium for humor because it lends itself so well to the expression of made-up words, funny rhymes, and aptly told punch lines. Another advantage is that a funny poem, like a good joke, can usually be easily memorized, which makes for a smooth delivery by young humorists.

Outrageously funny verse is offered in Shel Silverstein's *Where the Sidewalk Ends*, a volume that will be grabbed up by children of all ages. Among the characters boys and girls will meet are Jimmy Jet who turns into a television set, Ridiculous Rose who eats with her toes, Sarah Cynthia Sylvia Stout who will not take the garbage out, and silly young king who won't eat anything but peanut-butter sandwiches! Silverstein has added additional humor in his wry black-and-white line drawings.

William Cole's raucous *Beastly Boys and Ghastly Girls* is an anthology of wickedly merry, misbehaviorish poems featuring selections from the whimsical pens of Shel Silverstein, John Ciardi, and Lewis Carroll, among others. Droll drawings are by Tomi Ungerer. Another anthology to keep students amused is *My Tang's Tungled and Other Ridiculous Situations*, compiled by Sara and John E. Brewton and G. Meredith Blackburn III and illustrated in black-and-white line drawings by Graham Booth.

The title *Of Quirks, Quasars and Other Quirks: Quizzical Poems for the Supersonic Age*, also compiled by Sara and John E. Brewton and John Brewton Blackburn, is a clue to the wild and zany offerings of such master poets as John Updike, Ogden Nash, Eve Merriam, and Felice Holman. The subjects range from atomic bombs, pollution, and organic foods to computers and water beds! Although geared to middle and upper graders, the poems will appeal to younger children as they listen to the selections you read. Line drawings are by Quentin Blake.

BEAR HUMOR

Many kinds of animals have been the object and subject of humor, and bears are no exception. They seem to have a comic quality that appeals to authors, illustrators, and children alike. To capitalize on that interest, ask the students to seek out "bear" titles in the library or at home. Then place the books in a reading corner with a display of toy bears. Chances are that several boys or girls will welcome the chance to bring in their "teddys." The following three titles are perfect for reading aloud.

An old standby and perennial favorite, *Bears* by Ruth Krauss, was first published in 1948. This verse, containing only 16 words, will move the youngsters to memorize it in no time at all. Pictures are by Phyllis Rowland.

There isn't one word at all in *The Bear and the Fly*, illustrated in full color by Paula Winter, but it is action-packed. A fly interrupts a tranquil family of bears at breakfast, and soon Papa disrupts the house trying to swat it. This delightful book is just the thing to get students talking, describing, and acting. They can also write captions related to particular pages. Another marvelous title is *Bearymore*, written and illustrated by Don Freeman. A showbusiness bear has trouble hibernating and uses his sleeplessness to dream up a circus act.

Before, during, or after these treats, have a honey party. Many simple recipes for honey dishes can be found in *The Pooh Cookbook* by Virginia H. Ellison, with illustrations by Ernest H. Shepard. This is a good way to introduce or reintroduce the now senior citizen, Pooh, to add to the bevy of newer bear characters.

GET IT? GET IT?

Many budding stand-up comics relish reading and/or telling one-liners. The quickest of quickies can be found in *Daffynitions*, compiled by Charles Keller, with duotone cartoon illustrations by F. A. Fitzgerald. A daffynition, according to the flap copy of the book, is a "loony line devised to make the most ordinary word absurd." In alphabetical order, this romp takes us from "A/announce/one-sixteenth of a pound" to "Z/zoo-keeper/ a critter-sitter."

Math riddles and puzzles to amuse and challenge are contained in *Nutty Number Riddles* by Rose Wyler and Eva-Lee Baird, with whimsical two-color illustrations by Whitney Darrow, Jr. These mathematical teasers are perfect for a weekly riddle contest.

Four riddle books provide more material to chuckle and groan with. *The Monster Riddle Book* and *Space: A Fact and Riddle Book*, both by Jane Sarnoff and Reynold Ruffins, are attractively designed with four-color illustrations. *Ji-Nongo-Nongo Means Riddles* is an unusual collection of over 40 African riddles culled from 11 of the great tribes of Africa, including the Yoruba, the Masai, and the Kanuri, by Verna Aardema, with excellent duotone illustrations by Jerry Pinkney. *Biggest Riddle Book in the World* by Joseph Rosenbloom, with line drawings by Joyce Behr, offers 19 sections and includes a madcap index of subjects from "Abel" to "Zombies!"

JOKE FEST

After children have explored the ways in which books make us smile, they can entertain each other with a classroom joke fest. Volunteers can read or tell favorite jokes, puns, poems, or funny stories while a group of student judges rate audience laughter. Or have the children design a laugh response system by assigning point values to a "knee-slapper," a "belly-laugh," a "ribtickler" and a mere "ha-ha."

VOILÀ

Books of magic how-tos are exciting and challenging and offer children the chance to indulge in some theatricality. The following titles might even spark the interests and talents of a future Houdini.

Add some rhythm to magic study and performance by teaching the class part of the song "Magic to Do" from the Broadway hit, *Pippin*, available on the Motown Record label. The lyrics are included on the album, available at most record stores.

Funny Magic: Easy Tricks for Young Magicians by Rose Wyler and Gerald Ames gives young readers directions for performing easy sleight-of-hand tricks, using easily obtainable materials. Illustrations are by Tālavaldis Stubis.

In addition to suggestions for staging a major magic show, *Abracadabra!* by Barbara Seulig, includes nine program ideas ranging from short (8 to 12 minutes) to long (about 20 minutes) productions. Added bonuses to this volume for middle-grade sorcerers are listings of magic dealers throughout the country, magic magazines, and a bibliography of books about stage magic.

For mature magicians, there are two excellent titles to suggest—*The Great Mysto... That's You* by Laurence B. White, Jr.; and *Pure Magic: The Sleight-of-Hand Book of Dazzling Tricks and Captivating Routines* by Henry Gross. " ... *Mysto* gives complete, entertaining advice on performing trickery, starting with the simple and progressing to planning and staging a real show that will leave the audience mystified and amazed. The author has been a magician since he was 13 years old. Black-and-white drawings are by Will Winslow. *Pure Magic* contains black-and-white photographs along with complete step-by-step directions for basic sleights, each of which can be performed with familiar objects found around the house. Tricks include palming coins, performing magic with silk scarves, napkins, thimbles, balls, and cards. An index is appended.

Steer dedicated magic buffs to *Escape King: The Story of Harry Houdini* by John Ernst, with black-and-white illustrations by Ray Abel; and *The Great Houdini* by Anne Edwards, with black-and-white drawings by Joseph Ciardiello. These are biographies that give a fascinating account of one of the greatest magicians and escape artists of all times. In addition to the illustrations in the Ernst book, three actual photographs of the "king" himself appear.

REFERENCES[1]

Aardema, Verna. *Ji-Nongo Means Riddles.* Four Winds, 1978.

Brewton, Sara, John E. Brewton, and G. Meredith Blackburn III. *My Tang's Tungled and Other Ridiculous Situations.* Crowell, 1973.

Brewton, Sara, John E. Brewton, and John Brewton Blackburn. *Of Quirks, Quasars and Other Quirks: Quizical Poems for the Supersonic Age.* Crowell, 1977.

Clark, David Allen. *Jokes, Puns and Riddles.* Doubleday, 1968.

[1]See Appendix for publishers' complete addresses.

Cole, William, comp. *Beastly Boys and Ghastly Girls.* Collins + World, 1974; Dell paperback.

Edwards, Anne. *The Great Houdini.* Putnam, 1977.

Ellison, Virginia H. *The Pooh Cookbook.* Dutton, 1969; Dell paperback.

Emrich, Duncan. *The Hodgepodge Book.* Four Winds, 1972.

———. *The Nonsense Book of Riddles, Rhymes, Tongue-Twisters, Puzzles and Jokes from American Folklore.* Four Winds, 1970.

———. *The Whim-Wham Book.* Four Winds, 1975.

Ernst, John. *Escape King: The Story of Harry Houdini.* Prentice-Hall, 1975; also available in paperback.

Freeman, Don. *Bearymore.* Viking, 1976.

Gross, Henry. *Pure Magic: The Sleight-of-Hand Book of Dazzling Tricks and Captivating Routines.* Scribner, 1978.

Keller, Charles. *Daffynitions.* Prentice-Hall, 1976; also available in paperback.

Krauss, Ruth. *Bears.* Harper & Row, 1948; Scholastic paperback.

Parish, Peggy. *Amelia Bedelia and the Surprise Shower.* Harper & Row, 1966; Scholastic paperback.

Rosenbloom, Joseph. *Biggest Riddle Book in the World.* Sterling, 1976.

Sarnoff, Jane, and Reynold Ruffins. *The Monster Riddle Book*, rev. ed. Scribner, 1978.

———. *Space: A Fact and Riddle Book.* Scribner, 1978.

Schwartz, Alvin. *Cross Your Fingers, Spit in Your Hat: Superstitions and Other Beliefs.* Lippincott, 1974; also available in paperback.

———. *Tomfoolery: Trickery and Foolery with Words.* Lippincott, 1973; Bantam paperback.

———. *A Twister of Twists, A Tangler of Tongues: Tongue Twisters.* Lippincott, 1972; also available in paperback.

———. *Whoppers: Tall Tales and Other Lies.* Lippincott, 1975, also available in paperback.

———. *Witcracks: Jokes and Jests from American Folklore.* Lippincott, 1973; also available in paperback.

Seulig, Barbara. *Abracadabra!* Messner, 1975; Archway paperback.

Silverstein, Shel. *Where the Sidewalk Ends.* Harper & Row, 1974.

White, Laurence B, Jr. *The Great Mysto . . . That's You.* Addison-Wesley, 1975.

———. *Science Games.* Addison-Wesley, 1975.

———. *Science Toys.* Addison-Wesley, 1975.

———. *Science Tricks.* Addison-Wesley, 1975.

———. *Science Puzzles.* Addison-Wesley, 1975.

Winter, Paula. *The Bear and the Fly.* Crown, 1976.

Wyler, Rose and Gerald Ames. *Funny Magic: Easy Tricks for Young Magicians.* Parent's Magazine, 1977.

———. *Prove It!* Addison-Wesley, 1975; Scholastic paperback.

———. *Science Riddles.* Scholastic paperback.

Wyler, Rose, and Eva-Lee Baird. *Nutty Number Riddles.* Doubleday, 1974.

Games:
Playing via books

Whether children are learning a new game, sharing an old
one, or teaching friends the rules of a favorite pastime, they
will love leafing through books on the subject—from history to
how-to. You might want to poll your class first to find out what
types of games they are currently playing. This will give you a
clue as to their favorites and where to go from there.

CULTURAL AND HISTORICAL BACKGROUND

To unearth some intriguing background information on
games, try the professional text, *Children's Games in Street
and Playground* by Iona and Peter Opie. After studying responses from more than 10,000 children in England, Scotland,
and Wales, the Opies have compiled details on how games are
played, the rhymes and sayings children repeat while playing
them, the different names under which games are played, and
highly informative notes on individual histories. Mature upper-grade readers can dip into this volume to learn about the
diverse and exciting origins and cultural influences of the
games they play. They will also become acquainted with a wide
variety of unusual games such as "Ghosties in the Garrett" and
"Backofenkraucher," which involve movement as well as dramatic action.

GAME PLANS

You might set aside a period each week to have student volunteers report on favorite games. They can share a new game with the class, discuss its strategies, research and report on origins and statistics, or even design and plan an original game. Your school's physical education instructor can be an indispensable human resource for executing many of the children's ideas. The following titles can aid children in compiling information and provide fun-filled reading.

A surefire choice for primary graders is *Games (and How to Play Them),* written and illustrated by Anne Rockwell. The volume offers 43 popular indoor and outdoor games that can be played with simple rules and directions, little or no equipment, and no adult supervision. Of special interest are the visual delights in the vibrant watercolor-and-ink illustrations of animal players; for example, pandas engaging in "Chinese Hop" and elephants in "Giant Steps."

STREET GAMES

H. E. Bates, a sociologist, once stated, "There is no doubt that the First World War and the coming of the motor car killed, I suppose forever, the playing of street games in this country." But if Bates could see the sidewalks and streets of many communities today, he might quickly change his mind.

Games in the Street by Rachel Gallagher, photographed by Jaydie Putterman, describes more than 15 of these pastimes. It includes instructions, variations of play, a bit of their history, a bibliography and index, and a chapter on how to choose "who goes first."

Games, Games, Games/Juegos, Juegos, Juegos by Ruben Sandoval is a collection of street games played by children living in Mexican-American barrios. It is designed "to help maintain the continuity between the games of Mexico and the newer ones played in the barrios of California . . . and to help preserve a truly bilingual and bicultural tradition in the United States." David Strick's lively black-and-white photographs of children playing tag, ball games, marbles, circle games, and others are captioned with easy-to-follow directions. English and Spanish are interwoven throughout the text, and respective translations appear in an appendix.

TILES, PUZZLES, MONOPOLIES, PIECES

When it is raining outside, or when thermometers rise to sweltering levels or descend to freezing degrees, children often turn to popular indoor games such as dominoes, crossword puzzles, Monopoly, and chess. Several entertaining fact-filled volumes for older students can add to their enjoyment and help improve playing skills.

The Domino Book by Frederick Berndt, notes that this 200-year-old-plus game is played the world over. Readers will learn the origins of the name of the game and the game itself, terms used in playing, and rules for over 175 versions, many invented by the author.

Since the very first one appeared in print in December 21, 1913, in the *New York Herald,* crosswords have become one of the most popular of all pastimes. According to a Gallup poll, the crossword, an American invention by Arthur Wynne, is our leading sedentary recreation, claiming more than 30 million fans in the United States, more than checkers, chess, bingo, poker, or bridge. In *Crossword Puzzles: Their History and Their Cult,* author Roger Millington displays a wealth of knowledge about "the craze," including stories about people who design puzzles and a representative sampling of some of the more unusual varieties—the double crostic, crypotogram, and the world's toughest puzzle series.

The Monopoly Book: Strategies and Tactics of the World's Most Popular Game by Maxine Brady traces the history and development of the game, details the rules, and describes strategies for becoming the richest player on the board.

Two books on chess will be welcomed by young devotees of the game. *Chess for Children Step-by-Step: A New Easy Way to Learn the Game,* written by International Grandmaster William Lombardy and Bette Marshall, is based on the idea that if you really understand how each individual chess piece moves, you can quickly understand the total game. Instructions for simple, easy-to-follow moves are offered, along with diagrams and many black-and-white photographs by Marshall. The internationally recognized algebraic notation is simply explained. A different approach is offered in *Make Your Own Chess Set* by David Carroll. This volume provides instructions for making 25 wildly unique chess sets from a myriad of inexpensive and easy-to-find materials, such as screws, plumbing parts, hose fixtures, gumdrops, and nuts. The book includes an introduction to the history of chess and its pieces and is illustrated with black-and-white photographs.

Combining books and games can be a skillful, strategic move in your classroom. By capitalizing on one of the universal interests of children, you can help avid players become enthusiastic readers.

REFERENCES[1]

Berndt, Frederick. *The Domino Book.* Nelson, 1974.

Brady, Maxine. *The Monopoly Book: Strategies and Tactics of the World's Most Popular Game.* McKay, 1974; also available in paperback.

Carroll, David. *Make Your Own Chess Set.* Prentice-Hall, 1974; also available in paperback.

Gallagher, Rachel. *Games in the Street.* Four Winds, 1976.

Lombardy, William, and Bette Marshall. *Chess for Children Step-by-Step: A New Easy Way to Learn the Game.* Little, Brown, 1977; also available in paperback.

Millington, Roger. *Crossword Puzzles: Their History and Their Cult.* Nelson, 1975.

Opie, Iona, and Peter Opie. *Children's Games in Street and Playground.* Oxford, 1969.

Rockwell, Anne. *Games (and How We Play Them).* Crowell, 1973.

Sandoval, Ruben. *Games, Games, Games/Juegos, Juegos, Juegos.* Doubleday, 1977.

[1]See Appendix for publishers' complete addresses.

Team them up with sports books

In *Bruce and Chrystie Jenner's Guide to Family Fitness*, the Olympic decathlon winner and his wife state, "Lifetime sports are very important, but unfortunately they are one area in our lives that have been neglected, especially at younger ages ... young children should be exposed to sports they can play for the rest of their lives." Since most girls and boys do have some interest in one sport or another, you can capitalize on their enthusiasm via books about sports. Such books enhance reading experiences as well as stress the importance that sports play in physical development. Begin by asking children to name their favorite sports. Use their responses as a guide for gathering books and related materials.

A good title to have on hand is *The Last Legal Spitball and Other Little-Known Facts About Sports* by Barbara Seulig. This 79-page treasury of frivolous facts, figures, and anecdotes is sure to delight youngsters of all ages and is ideal for reluctant readers, since most of the entries are only a few sentences long. Start an ongoing sports bulletin board by posting a few of the facts from this book. Then encourage the children to add to the display by researching additional information about their favorite sports, using newspapers, magazines, or a compilation such as *Guinness Book of World Records,* edited by Norris McWhirter. Those who share a common interest in one sport could work in teams. Set aside one portion of the bulletin board for newspaper or magazine clippings about current happenings in the sports world. Several student sportcasters could be in charge of updating the board writing features or interviewing class sports personalities.

Members of your class could also interview older students, brothers and sisters, or the physical education teacher to learn game rules and some of the fine points of technique about their favorite sport. Older researchers could delve into the history and origin of a particular sport or focus on its famous personalities—historical or contemporary. Try to schedule time for students to share their findings with the class via oral reports, panel discussions, or demonstrations.

You might extend the sports mania to mathematics. Discuss various scoring techniques or percentages and averages related to popular teams and players. Tie in the concept of probability by suggesting that interested students evaluate information on the two World Series teams and predict the winner.

SPORTS CONTEMPORARIES

There is an abundance of sports biographies for readers at all levels. After the students have read one or several, they might plan and create minibiography booklets of their favorite athletes. These can be illustrated with photographs cut from newspapers or magazines and include the children's artwork.

Four easy-to-read books in the popular "Crowell Biography" series written by Kenneth Rudeen include *Roberto Clemente,* illustrated by Frank Mullins, about the Puerto Rican star elected to the Baseball Hall of Fame after his untimely death in an airplane crash while delivering supplies to Nicaraguan earthquake victims; *Jackie Robinson*, about the first black to play major league baseball, illustrated by Richard Cuffari; *Wilt Chamberlain,* about the famous basketball player, also illustrated by Mullins; and *Muhammad Ali*, illustrated by George Ford, about the boxer who became the world heavyweight champion at the age of 22.

Another attractive series is the "Sports Star" books by S. H. Burchard. Included in the wide variety of titles are biographies of *Pelé*, the greatest soccer player in the world; *Nadia Comaneci*, the Romanian gymnast who won a bronze medal and three gold medals at the 1976 Olympic Games in Montreal, Canada; *Bob Griese,* the Miami Dolphins quarterback; and *Dorothy Hamill*, one of the few skaters ever to win the United

States Championship and an Olympic gold medal all in one year—1976. All of the books in this series are illustrated with black-and-white photographs and line drawings by Paul Frame, are available in high-quality paperback editions, and are designed with large print. These titles will appeal to all avid sports fans, including reluctant readers.

For mature readers, *Breaking In,* compiled and edited by Lawrence T. Lorimer, gives first-person accounts on nine athletes who aspired to become champions. Each person describes his or her experiences, focusing on a crucial turning point in their lives. Fascinating facts in nine lives are detailed. Included are Althea Gibson, the tennis champ who grew up on the streets of Harlem; Rube Marquard, who ran away from home at 16 to play baseball; and actor Anthony Quinn, who was once a boxer.

SPORTS FICTION

Harper & Row's "Sports I Can Read Books" written and illustrated in color by Leonard Kessler are geared for beginning readers. The four titles include *Kick, Pass and Run,* a hilarious tale about a group of animals that try their skill at football; *On Your Mark, Get Set, Go,* in which the same characters hold their own Olympic games; *Last One in Is a Rotten Egg,* about swimming; and *Here Comes the Strikeout,* a baseball story which is also available in a Spanish edition, *Aqui Viene el Ponchado,* translated by Pura Belpré.

Ann McGovern's *Scram Kid!* sets a different tone. The story revolves around Joe, a young city boy, who yearns to play baseball but is turned away by the other boys. He fantasizes about getting even with the team by yelling such things as, "Go soak your head," and "Make like a drum and beat it!" The tale shows that being left out, getting angry about it, and then finding something else to do can all be part of a normal day—and life. The large picture-book format makes this a natural for story-hour use. Illustrations are by Nola Langner. Upper graders will enjoy the lively, first-person account of Laura in Julia First's *Flat on My Face.* Laura is not allowed to play on the Little League team because she is a girl, even though she loves the sport, is a fantastic third baser, and knows famous batting averages by heart!

Introduce your students to stories emphasizing sportsmanship and team effort with books by Matt Christopher and Alfred Slote, two popular authors for middle-grade readers. Several titles by Christopher are *The Year Mom Won the Pennant, The Kid Who Only Hit Homers,* and *Baseball Flyhawk,* all illustrated by Foster Caddell. Titles by Slote include *Matt Gargan's Boy, My Father, the Coach, The Biggest Victory,* and *Hang Tough, Paul Mather,* a sensitive novel about a Little League pitcher afflicted with an incurable blood disease who plays out his short season with dignity and courage. The title is also available in a Spanish edition, *¡Coraje, campeón!.* All of the above are exciting, realistic accounts that many children will set aside their bats and balls to read!

After some in-class sports involvement, you might initiate a "Classroom Hall of Fame." Suggest that the children nominate their favorite sports personalities and give speeches justifying each inclusion. Follow up with an election. Or establish a "Fiction Hall of Fame," encouraging the students to select favorite book characters to extol.

PLAYING THE GAMES

Upper-grade fans of the home run, touchdown, slam dunk, ace, and hole in one will flex their fingers through two volumes that deal with major sports. *How Sports Began* by Don Smith and Anne Marie Mueser, illustrated with black-and-white photographs, prints, and art reproductions, cites legends and facts about the origin of 19 athletic contests. There is something for everyone—from neophyte to pro—in the more complete *Sports and Games* by Harold Keith, which traces the history of 16 popular sports and games and gives up-to-date information on rules along with suggestions for improving playing techniques. Both volumes contain an index.

Although it may not be in the big leagues yet, Frisbee throwing is a number-one activity for many children. Information about this pie-pan-shaped plastic disc is detailed in *Frisbee Fun* by Margaret Poynter. Included are the history of this popular game, scientific facts about the Frisbee's flight, various throwing techniques, and contests to learn about and practice for. Children will also enjoy *Fabulous Frisbee* by Dorothy Childers Schmitz, an easy-to-read volume, illustrated with lively full-color photographs.

Several series of titles can also acquaint readers with the

rules of the games. Each of the titles in the "Sports for Me" series published by Lerner are easy-to-read, first-person accounts, dealing with techniques, terms, and game rules of such sports as baseball, gymnastics, hockey, skateboarding, skiing, soccer, tennis, and track. The last page of each volume contains a brief, one-paged glossary. Among the titles are *Skiing Is For Me* by Annette Jo Chappell and *Hockey Is For Me* by Lowell A. Dickmeyer, both with photographs by Alan Oddie. For a complete listing of series titles, write to the publisher for their catalog.

Five fact-filled titles make up the "Young People's Sport Dictionary Series," published in paperback under the logo Prentice-Hall Treehouse Paperbacks. They include *Illustrated Basketball Dictionary for Young People* by Steve Clark, illustrated by Frank Beginski; *Illustrated Hockey Dictionary for Young People* by Henry Walker, illustrated by Beginski; *Illustrated Football Dictionary for Young People* by Joseph Olgin, illustrated by Larry Sutton; *Illustrated Baseball Dictionary for Young People* by Walker, illustrated by Leonard Kessler; and *Illustrated Soccer Dictionary for Young People* by James S. Gardner, illustrated by David Ross. In dictionary format, each book contains terms used in the games; for example, in ... *Football* ..., entries run from "A/Advance to a two-yard line," to Z/Zone defense," along with brief explanations. Appended are additional facts including some of the sports "Greatest Players of All Times." Black-and-white line drawings illustrate the books.

Another series to look for is "Basic Strategy Books" published by Doubleday. Titles include *Basic Baseball Strategy* by S. H. Freeman, *Basic Field Hockey* by Lee Ann Williams, and two titles by Richard B. Lyttle focusing on volleyball and hockey.

SPORTS IN POETRY

Donald Anderson, a sixth-grade teacher in Las Vegas, Nevada, whets his students' poetry appetites with a sports-in-poetry bulletin board display. You can too!

A photo montage about a specific sport, along with several related sports poems, is created by the students. On the bulletin board is the following suggestion: "Make a photo montage yourself about a sport you like. Find a poem about the sport. Or write one yourself." Underneath the bulletin board, include a table display of books containing sports poems. Sources for upper grades are *Sprints and Distances: Sports in Poetry and the Poetry in Sports*, compiled by Lillian Morrison, with illustrations by Claire and John Ross; *Sports Poems*, edited by R. R. Knudson and P. K. Elbert; *Faces and Places: Poems for You*, selected by Lee Bennett Hopkins and Misha Arenstein; *Hosannah, the Home Run!: Poems About Sports*, selected by Alice Fleming; and *The Sidewalk Racer and Other Poems of Sports and Motion*, also by Morrison.

Almost every sport is represented in *Sprints and Distances.* Included are poems by ancient and modern writers ranging from Virgil to David McCord. The text is suited for mature readers. *Sports Poems* is a collection of over 100 poems by such authors as Cassius Clay, Carl Sandburg, and Emily Dickinson. The volume is divided into three sections: "Major Sports," "Minor Sports," and "Losers/Winners." An interesting feature of this anthology is the inclusion of facts and figures about sports events under the heading "Hall of Fame." Here is a book that will have strong appeal to students.

Faces and Places contains a section "Sports and Games"; 10 poems by contemporary poets are included. The poems are directed to children in grades four and up. *Hosannah, the Home Run!* includes 34 poems about 14 popular sports, illustrated with black-and-white action photographs. *The Sidewalk Racer* presents 38 original poems by Morrison, illustrated with black-and-white photographs. Surfers, sprinters, and sharpshooters will enjoy this unique edition.

REFERENCES[1]

Belpré, Pura, trans. *Aqui Viene el Ponchado*. Harper & Row, 1965; also available in paperback.

Burchard, S. H. *Bob Griese*, Harcourt, 1977; also available in paperback.

———. *Dorothy Hamill*. Harcourt, 1978; also available in paperback.

———. *Nadia Comaneci*. Harcourt, 1977; also available in paperback.

———.*Pelé*. Harcourt, 1976; also available in paperback.

Chappell, Annette Jo. *Skiing Is For Me.* Lerner, 1978.

Clark, Steve. *Illustrated Basketball Dictionary for Young People.* Prentice-Hall paperback.

Christopher, Matt. *Baseball Flyhawk.* Little, Brown, 1963.

[1]See Appendix for publishers' complete addresses.

————. *The Kid Who Only Hit Homers.* Little, Brown, 1972.

————. *The Year Mom Won the Pennant.* Little, Brown, 1968.

Dickmeyer, Lowell A. *Hockey Is For Me.* Lerner, 1978.

First, Julia. *Flat On My Face.* Prentice-Hall; Avon paperback.

Fleming, Alice, ed. *Hosannah, the Home Run!: Poems About Sports.* Little, Brown, 1972.

Freeman, S. H. *Basic Baseball Strategy.* Doubleday, 1965.

Gardner, James S. *Illustrated Soccer Dictionary for Young People.* Prentice-Hall paperback.

Hopkins, Lee Bennett and Misha Arenstein, eds. *Faces and Places: Poems For You.* Scholastic paperback.

Jenner, Bruce, and Chrystie Jenner. *Bruce and Chrystie Jenner's Guide to Family Fitness.* Grosset & Dunlap, 1978.

Keith, Harold. *Sports and Games.* Crowell, 1976.

Kessler, Leonard. *Here Comes the Strikeout.* Harper & Row, 1965; also available in paperback.

————. *Kick, Pass and Run.* Harper & Row, 1966; also available in paperback.

————. *Last One In Is A Rotten Egg.* Harper & Row, 1969.

————. *On Your Mark, Get Set, Go.* Harper & Row, 1972.

Knudson, R. R., and P. K. Elbert, eds. *Sports Poems.* Dell paperback.

Lorimer, Lawrence T., ed. *Breaking In.* Random House, 1974.

Lyttle, Richard B. *Basic Hockey Strategy.* Doubleday, 1976.

————. *Basic Volleyball Strategy.* Doubleday, 1978.

McGovern, Ann. *Scram Kid!* Viking, 1974.

McWhirter, Norris. *Guinness Book of World Records.* Bantam paperback.

Morrison, Lillian. *The Sidewalk Racer and Other Poems of Sports and Motion.* Lothrop, 1977.

————, ed. *Sprints and Distances: Sports in Poetry and the Poetry in Sports.* Crowell, 1965.

Olgin, Joseph. *Illustrated Football Dictionary for Young People.* Prentice-Hall paperback.

Poynter, Margaret. *Frisbee Fun.* Messner, 1977.

Rudeen, Kenneth. *Jackie Robinson.* Crowell, 1971; also available in paperback.

————. *Muhammad Ali.* Crowell, 1976.

————. *Roberto Clemente.* Crowell, 1974.

————. *Wilt Chamberlain.* Crowell, 1970; also available in paperback.

Schmitz, Dorothy Childers. *Fabulous Frisbee.* Crestwood, 1978.

Seulig, Barbara. *The Last Legal Spitball and Other Little-Known Facts About Sports.* Doubleday, 1975.

Slote, Alfred. *The Biggest Victory.* Lippincott, 1972; Avon paperback.

————. *¡Coraje, campeón!* Lippincott, 1979.

————. *Hang Tough, Paul Mather.* Lippincott, 1977; Avon paperback.

————. *Matt Gargan's Boy.* Lippincott, 1975; Avon paperback.

————. *My Father, the Coach.* Lippincott, 1972; Avon paperback.

Smith, Don, and Anne Marie Mueser. *How Sports Began.* Watts, 1977.

Walker, Henry. *Illustrated Baseball Dictionary for Young People.* Prentice-Hall paperback.

————. *Illustrated Hockey Dictionary for Young People.* Prentice-Hall paperback.

Williams, Lee Ann. *Basic Field Hockey Strategy.* Doubleday, 1978.

PART VII

Plants, Pets, and Beasts

28

Dinosaurs, monsters, and other beasts of weird

Books about dinosaurs, monsters, and other beasts of weird are quite appealing to children of all ages. To reap reading rewards using these popular subjects, try combining nonfiction with fiction. After discussing the differences between these two types of books, set up a book table display for each. Encourage the children to bring in other related books. Have them determine which books are factual and which are fictional. These books could be added to the appropriate table display.

DIG DINOSAUR FACTS

Dinosaurs are not sweeping the country anymore, but books about them are. I asked two youngsters why they are so popular.

A sixth grader told me, "They're safe! You know they can't get you, despite all the movies you see on television." A third-grade girl remarked that she liked reading books about dinosaurs "because dinosaurs are in history. And they're *stinked!*" Presumably she meant *extinct!*

Many youngsters, however, do misplace dinosaurs in time because science-fiction media often show humans and these creatures together. Clarifying this misconception is quite important.

The following nonfiction titles might spark an investigation on dinosaur history. As a follow-up, students could plan and paint a dinosaur mural, labeling the type of dinosaur each child drew and including some scientific data.

In *Dinosaur Time,* author Peggy Parish packs a great deal of information about 11 types of dinosaurs into 32 pages; their names are given along with a pronunciation key. These beasts, imaginatively illustrated by Arnold Lobel, roam the book's pages. Joanna Cole's *Dinosaur Story* recreates the lives of five dinosaurs, giving a few basic facts about each. Starting with the *brontosaurus,* the author relates one animal to another, ending with *Tyrannosaurus rex,* "the most terrible dinosaur there ever was." Ms. Cole carefully points out that information about the animals comes from studies of dinosaur bones, stressing that these are the best clues scientists have to work with. Detailed black-and-white sketches are done by Mort Kuntsler.

Tyrannosaurus Rex by Millicent Selsam gets full treatment in this factual account, illustrated with black-and-white photographs. The text describes the effort to reconstruct a *Tyrannosaurus rex* from fossilized bones found in Montana in 1901, and discusses resulting deductions about the creature's way of life. A short bibliography is appended.

Middle-grade readers will learn a great deal from the following titles.

M. Jean Craig's *Dinosaurs and More Dinosaurs* contains organized information depicting the evolution and specific characteristics of 46 kinds of dinosaurs. An added bonus of this dinosaur fancier's delight are the large, lifelike, and lavish two-color drawings by George Solonevich.

Laurence Pringle has written two enticing dinosaur books: *Dinosaurs and Their World,* an easy-to-read account on the rise and fall of the animals; and *Dinosaurs and People: Fossils, Facts and Fantasies,* which traces research on dinosaurs since the first discoveries of their fossils in Massachusetts in 1802. The volume also presents some of the startling new ideas now being considered regarding what they were really like. Both volumes illustrated with black-and-white photographs includes indexes.

What Really Happened to the Dinosaurs? by Daniel Cohen, with black-and-white illustrations by Harv Wells, examines the theories that scientists hold today to explain the intriguing mystery of the animals' extinction. Chapters include discoveries on climatic and habitat changes, competition, disease, and catastrophes. A brief bibliography and index are appended.

DINOSAUR FANTASIES

After students have discovered some of the fascinating facts about dinosaurs, let them savor the wild and wondrous settings, characters, and plots of fiction. When you feel they are ready, set their imaginations loose to conjure up some dinosaur tales of their own. Perhaps these titles will start young minds whirling: "The Ankylosaurus Who Sprained Her Ankylo," or "The Diplodocus Who Lives Upstairs."

An old standby for the primary grades is Syd Hoff's *Danny and the Dinosaur,* about a boy who spends an unforgettable day in the city with his friend, the museum dinosaur. This title is also available in Spanish, *Danielito y el Dinosauro,* translated by Pura Belpré. *Dinosaur's Homecoming Party* by Norma Klein is a humorous adventure, sprightly illustrated by James Marshall. When a dinosaur named Dinosaur moves into a new penthouse apartment in New York City, his friends—Octopus and Green Worm—plan a housewarming party during which unbelievable happenings occur.

Although Michael Foreman's *Dinosaurs and All That Rubbish* is designed as a picture book, it will appeal to all grade levels. The text is poetic; the illustrations large and imaginative. This is a dinosaur must!

If the Dinosaurs Came Back, written and illustrated by Bernard Most, relates a series of wishes and fantasies a young boy has if the beasts could pop up in contemporary times. The dinosaurs could "help build big skyscrapers, rescue kittens stuck in very tall trees," and so on. The beasts are portrayed in purple, red, and yellow coats, which might give impetus to some exciting classroom art lessons.

The Tyrannosaurus Game by Steven Kroll will encourage young readers to invent their own *tyrannosaurus* game. Jimmy, bored with the rain, starts a pass-along story with his classmates beginning with, "Last Saturday I was eating breakfast, when all of a sudden a *tyrannosaurus* came crashing through the window." Peggy picks up the story, adds something new to it and passes it on to Susan, who passes it on to Billy, and so forth. When the story reaches Phillip, he comes up with a preposterous ending—with a purple dinosaur sitting atop the Empire State Building à la King Kong. Joyous three-color illustrations are by Caldecott Award Honor Book winner Tomie de Paola.

Once children clearly understand the difference between nonfiction and fiction, it's a safe step from dinosaur tales to books about fictitious beasts.

FEAST ON BEASTS

Undoubtedly the most beloved monsters in children's literature are the wild things created by the incomparable Maurice Sendak in *Where the Wild Things Are.* Spark creative dramatics ideas by using the second filmstrip of the book available through Weston Woods, or the colorful 29" X 41" poster featuring a scene from the book available through Scholastic Book Services.

"The Little Monster" is just one tale in the easy-to-read little book by Ruth Krauss entitled *The Little King, the Little Queen, the Little Monster and Other Stories You Can Make Up Yourself.* The author's simple and funny line drawings might inspire children to write and illustrate a story of their own.

In *The Cereal Box* by David McPhail, a box of "Winkies" contains the wildest assortment of premiums that ever appeared at any breakfast table, including a leaping frog, a huge snake, and a green monster! After hearing this story, children might enjoy trying to determine what is inside a homemade "Touch Box." Place a variety of "feeling things" in a covered box, seal it, and cut out a hole in the top or side so that the children can reach in to feel the different objects. Have them guess what the objects are using only their sense of touch. After guessing, the child can lift out the object to see its true identity —and then put the object back in the box. This activity will aid youngsters in critical thinking.

You might read aloud Judith Viorst's delightful *My Mama Says There Aren't Any Zombies, Ghosts, Vampires, Creatures, Demons, Monsters, Fiends, Goblings or Things,* illustrated by Kay Chorao. This book will no doubt generate lively class discussions about the real and the imagined. In the words of the author, "Sometimes even mamas make mistakes."

Steer middle-grade readers to the trilogy of monster tales, *A-Haunting We Will Go, Witching Time,* and *Monsters, Ghoulies and Creepy Creatures,* volumes of stories and poems selected by Lee Bennett Hopkins, illustrated in black-and-white line drawings by Vera Rosenberry. Each of the books contains a wide variety of both contemporary tales as well as those culled from folklore throughout the world.

Older students might be stimulated to create their own fantastic beasts in a variety of media after reading *Gargoyles, Monsters and Other Beasts* by Shay Rieger. Black-and-white photographs show "beastly" sculpture from the past as well as children's artwork inspired by the fantastical.

REFERENCE READING

Beasts of weird abound in both classic and contemporary works of fantasy. The three volumes discussed below are compendia of information about mythological and supernatural beings and good resources for the reading shelf.

In *The Impossible People: A History Natural and Unnatural of Beings Terrible and Wonderful,* Georges McHargue analyzes and describes the chief mythological people. The volume is illustrated with black-and-white drawings by Frank Bozzo. Formally titled *The Glass Harmonica,* Barbara Ninde Byfield's volume has been reprinted in a large-sized paperbound edition under the title *The Book of Weird.* This lexicon describes and defines such things as crones, vampires, and demons.

Almost everyone has heard of the Abominable Snowman, but what about the "Abominable Chicken Man of Oklahoma"? Or the hodag—the man-eating creature of the Wisconsin swamps? Daniel Cohen's *Monsters, Giants, and Little Men from Mars: An Unnatural History of the Americas* is an account of some of the beasties who reputedly lurk around and about our continent. The volume contains 31 black-and-white photographs.

Mature readers will enjoy the classic tale of one of the greatest monsters of all time—*Frankenstein.* This tour-de-force, written by Mary Shelley, is available in paperback from Scholastic and also on record or cassette from Miller-Brody.

POETRY PEG

Dinosaur Funny Bones and *Dinosaur Do's and Don't's* by Jean Burt Polhamus are sure to be enjoyed by children of all ages. The rhymes—21 in each book—lampoon the characteristics of the big-named, little-brained creatures in terse verse. In addition to the rhymes, there is a pronunciation guide, factual descriptions of the animals, indices, and a bibliography for children interested in further exploration of dinosaur facts. Amusing illustrations are done by Mamoru Funai.

"When Dinosaurs Ruled the Earth," by Patricia Hubbell, is a favorite poem with children. The selection appeared in *The Apple Vendor's Fair* which is now out of print, but you can find the poem in *To Look At Any Thing,* an anthology of poetry selected by Lee Bennett Hopkins, with black-and-white photographs by John Earl. Boys and girls can practice pronouncing dinosaur names by repeating the poem's refrain: "Brontosaurus, diplodocus, gentle trachodon. . . ."

Ted Hughes's *Nessie the Monster* is a verse tale based on the Loch Ness Monster who supposedly lurks in Loch Ness in northern Scotland. The witty ditty is illustrated by Jan Pyk. Two short verses appear in *Egg Thoughts and Other Frances Songs* by Russell Hoban in his poem, "Songs for Television Shows I would Like to See." One is about "Doctor Vampire," the other, "Mister Skeleton."

Nightmares: Poems to Trouble Your Sleep includes 12 haunting poems by the masterful, Jack Prelutsky, featuring such creatures as "The Bogeyman," "The Vampire," "The Werewolf," and "The Ogre." Excellent black-and-white scratchboard drawings by Arnold Lobel add to this ghoulish delight.

REFERENCES[1]

Belpré, Pura, trans. *Danielito y el Dinosaurio.* Harper & Row, 1958.

Byfield, Barbara Ninde. *The Book of Weird.* Doubleday, paperback.

Cohen, Daniel. *Monsters, Giants, and Little Men from Mars: An unnatural History of the Americas.* Doubleday, 1975.

———. *What Really Happened to the Dinosaurs?* Dutton, 1977.

Cole, Joanna. *Dinosaur Story.* Morrow, 1974.

Craig, M. Jean. *Dinosaurs and More Dinosaurs.* Four Winds, 1968; Scholastic paperback.

Foreman, Michael. *Dinosaurs and All That Rubbish.* Crowell, 1972.

Hoban, Russell. *Egg Thoughts and Other Frances Songs.* Harper & Row, 1972.

Hoff, Syd. *Danny and the Dinosaur.* Harper & Row, 1958: also available in paperback.

Hopkins, Lee Bennett, ed. *A-Haunting We Will Go.* Whitman, 1977.

———, ed. *Monsters, Ghoulies and Creepy Creatures.* Whitman, 1977.

————, ed. *To Look At Any Thing.* Harcourt, 1978.

————, ed. *Witching Time.* Whitman, 1977.

Hughes, Ted. *Nessie the Monster.* Bobbs-Merrill, 1974.

Klein, Norma. *Dinosaur's Housewarming Party.* Crown, 1974.

Kroll, Steven. *The Tyrannosaurus Game.* Holiday House, 1976.

Krauss, Ruth. *The Little King, the Little Queen, the Little Monster and Other Stories You Can Make Up Yourself.* Scholastic paperback.

McHargue, Georges. *The Impossible People: A History Natural and Unnatural of Beings Terrible and Wonderful.* Holt, Rinehart and Winston 1972; Dell paperback.

McPhail, David. *The Cereal Box.* Little, Brown, 1974.

Most, Bernard. *If the Dinosaurs Came Back.* Harcourt, 1978.

Parish, Peggy. *Dinosaur Time.* Harper & Row, 1974; Scholastic paperback.

Polhamus, Jean Burt. *Dinosaur Do's and Don't's.* Prentice-Hall, 1975; also available in paperback.

————. *Dinosaur Funny Bones.* Prentice-Hall, 1974; also available in paperback.

Prelutsky, Jack. *Nightmares: Poems to Trouble Your Sleep.* Greenwillow, 1976.

Pringle, Laurence. *Dinosaurs and People: Fossils, Facts and Fantasies.* Harcourt, 1978.

————. *Dinosaurs and Their World.* Harcourt, 1968; also available in paperback.

Rieger, Shay. *Gargoyles, Monsters and Other Beasts.* Lothrop, 1972.

Selsam, Millicent. *Tyrannosaurus Rex.* Harper & Row, 1978.

Sendak, Maurice. *Where the Wild Things Are.* Harper & Row, 1963; Scholastic paperback.

Shelley, Mary. *Frankenstein.* Scholastic paperback.

Viorst, Judith. *My Mama Says There Aren't any Zombies, Ghosts, Vampires, Creatures, Demons, Monsters, Fiends, Goblins or Things.* Atheneum, 1973; also available in paperback.

29

Sequined salvia and "fonzied" ficus:
The greening of reading

Leaf greenery is a subject of interest to students of all ages. To get things growing—seeds and young minds—plan grow-it-yourself projects with the students. Before, during, and after cultivation sessions, you can intertwine these living things with a variety of books.

Begin such a project by having the children bring to class different kinds of seeds and some potting soil. Paper cups or half-pint milk cartons make perfect planters. They are easy to collect, and the children can cover them with construction paper and decorate them any way they want. In one classroom I visited, I really did see a sequin-covered container of salvia and a picture of the popular Fonzie, pasted on a pot of ficus!

Before planting, caution the children about using too much or too little soil, planting too deeply or too closely to the sides of the container, and drowning seedlings with too much water. When planting is complete, have each child prepare a chart, noting the name of the plant, the date, and the type of seed planted. Have them record the plants' growth in both English and metric measurements. A hand magnifying glass is a useful item for "pot watching." Or students may want to start a single "class plant." Something that reaches relatively great heights or lengths will make measurement sessions more fun.

PRIMARY PLANTERS

While everyone is waiting for the first dots of green to appear, you might read or have the children share two perennial "oldies but goodies." *Seeds and More Seeds* by Millicent Selsam, illustrated by Tomi Ungerer, tells the story of Benny, a young lad who tries growing a stone, a pebble, a marble, and a seed. When only the seed sprouts, Benny becomes "seed crazy," planting as many as he can find. As he learns more and more about these tiny storehouses of life, so do young readers. No primary classroom is complete without at least one copy of *The Carrot Seed* by Ruth Krauss, illustrated by Crockett Johnson. This joyously illustrated text relates a young boy's determination to grow a carrot even though everyone says, "It won't come up."

Two other titles help convey the idea that a plant's effort to find a place in the sun isn't always an easy task. In *The Tiny Seed,* written and illustrated by Eric Carle, a seed and its siblings fly on the autumn wind far around the world. But many never make it. One falls into the water and drowns; another is eaten by a bird. Despite these hardships, one tiny seed finds a soil sanctuary and grows into the biggest, most beautiful flower that people, birds, and insects have ever seen. When autumn comes again, the flower's seed pod opens and "out come many tiny seeds that quickly sail far away on the wind." The book's large format makes it a perfect selection for story hours. Glorious full-color illustrations will inspire children to create collage-type drawings of their own.

A simple tale of a seed lying deep in the dark ground is appropriately titled *The Seed* by Ann Cameron. One day it awakens, begins to grow, and finally becomes a little tree. Haunting water-color paintings by Beth Cannon add to the sensitivity of this story.

PLOTS AND POTS

Few feelings can match a child's pride in nurturing a plant. Several nonfiction titles can further encourage do-it-yourself activities and enhance learnings about living things. The three volumes discussed below will spark girls and boys to become active and interested "green-thumbers!"

Younger children will delight in *How to Grow A Jelly Glass*

Farm by Kathy Mandy, with full-color stylized illustration by Joe Toto. The author points out that: "To have a farm, you don't need tractors or plows or acres of land. All you need are a few things you can find in your kitchen and other corners of the house." Fourteen simple-to-execute projects are explained, such as "Green Feet," encouraging children to plant grass seed in an old sneaker, and "Pie Pan Gulch," suggesting that youngsters grow a cactus garden in an old tinfoil pie plate or pan.

Middle and upper graders will find complete directions for growing "no-fail" house plants in *Plant Fun: Ten Easy Plants to Grow* by Anita Holmes Soucie. There is a chapter on each of the 10 plants, plus handy gardening tips and a five-page glossary. Illustrations in black-and-white are by Grambs Miller.

Many mathematics and science activities can be tied in with growing plants indoors. Seymour Simon's *Projects With Plants: A Science Work Book,* offers 27 clearly described projects that will introduce young experimenters to basic scientific terminology and procedures related to plant life. Readers will find out what kinds of plants eat animals, what types of plants can grow their way through a maze, and which prefer symphonic music to jazz. Children will enjoy finding the answers to these and other questions in this volume with activities designed to reveal basic facts about the growth and nourishment of plant life. Black-and-white drawings are by Lynn Sweat.

SOPHISTICATED GARDENERS

Older children can combine the best of botany and social studies via a World Plant Hunt. Ask them to bring in different kinds of houseplants, research their characteristics, and pinpoint their original locations by using maps, globes, and reference books. Then they can compare plants from two different environments and speculate about what would happen if the locations were changed. For example, cacti are common to American desert regions. The exotic-looking "prayer plant"— the *Maranta*—flourishes in Brazilian rain forests. What would happen if this plant was forced to endure the living conditions of cacti?

Other areas of the world have given us several fairly common houseplants. From Africa come *Dracaena* and the African violet; from Asia and the Pacific Islands, *Ficus* (the rubber plant) and the Norfolk Island Pine, which resembles our traditional

Christmas tree; from Australia, the kangaroo vine or *Cissus antarctica,* which is similar in appearance to the maple.

Offer advanced readers titles that will aid their quests for all-season plant information and sharpen such skills as following directions, observing, keeping records, drawing conclusions, measuring, and graphing. *Plants for Pots: Projects for Indoor Gardens* by D. X. Fenten, presents year-round gardening projects. The possibilities range from avocado pits, pineapple tops, and fruit pits to unusual specimens like the spider plant (*Chlorophytum elatum*). "Twelve Months of Indoor Gardening," an excellent chapter, takes readers through seasonal plantings, including Coleus in the spring and live miniature Christmas trees in the winter. A glossary, index, and a very helpful name and pronunciation list are included. Illustrations are by Penelope Naylor.

An attractively designed how-to book for the beginning gardener is *A Gardening Book: Indoors and Outdoors,* written and illustrated by Anne Batterberry Walsh. A list is provided for each activity, detailing what will be needed, where to find or buy it, how to do each step, and how to follow through. Ideas range from the fun of building a terrarium and a garden grown from kitchen scraps to eating vegetables and herbs grown in garden plots or on a doorstep. A glossary is included.

Grow A Plant Pet: The Care and Feeding of Healthy Happy Plants, written and illustrated by Virginie Fowler Elbert, stresses basic plant care. Chapter 9, "Plant Projects To Try," cites specific methods for training plants and vines and cultivating various types of indoor gardens. The following chapter, "Plants to Choose From," is a pictorial guide to many of the in- and out-of-door plants one finds in stores—from African violets to zinnias—with complete descriptions of each plant and the information needed to grow it.

FOR ALL GREEN THUMBS

Nothing beats the pride of giving and the joy of receiving a handmade gift, so encourage the children to share the fruits— or leaves—of their labors. They can give plants or cuttings to special people on special occasions or for no occasion at all! What librarian, nurse, school secretary, principal, custodian, or parent wouldn't appreciate a sprout of one kind or another?

A whimsical bookmark—"Books About Plants and Growing

Things"—is a place-holding present you can give that will please youngsters. One side features a two-color illustration by Tomie de Paola; the reverse lists 15 fiction and nonfiction titles for further reading. The bookmarks are available in packages of 100 from The Children's Book Council.

The world's gardens, forests, and fields have inspired many authors and poets. Older children can find some of these writers' famous "quotable quotes" by turning to the entries for "Flower," "Plant," and "Tree" in the index of *Bartlett's Familiar Quotations* by John Bartlett. When they find excerpts that they like in the text, they can copy them on small pieces of paper and attach them to their plant containers. For example, this quote from Sir Thomas Pope Blount, seventeenth-century English politician and writer, would do any plant proud: "Every fiber of a plant ... can—if duly considered—read us lectures. . . ."

REFERENCES[1]

Bartlett, John. *Bartlett's Familiar Quotations.* Little, Brown, 1968.

Cameron, Ann. *The Seed.* Pantheon, 1975.

Carle, Eric. *The Tiny Seed.* Crowell, 1970.

Elbert, Virginie Fowler. *Grow A Plant Pet: The Care and Feeding of Healthy Happy Plants.* Doubleday, 1977.

Fenten, D. X. *Plants for Pots: Projects for Indoor Gardening.* Lippincott, 1969.

Krauss, Ruth. *The Carrot Seed.* Harper & Row, 1945.

Mandy, Kathy, *How to Grow A Jelly Glass Farm.* Pantheon, 1974.

Selsam, Millicent. *Seeds and More Seeds.* Harper & Row, 1959.

Simon, Seymour. *Projects with Plants: A Science Work Book.* Watts, 1973.

Soucie, Anita Holmes. *Plant Fun: Ten Easy Plants to Grow.* Four Winds, 1974.

Walsh, Anne Batterberry. *A Gardening Book: Indoors and Outdoors.* Atheneum, 1976.

[1]See Appendix for publishers' complete addresses.

30

A shark is not a jaw:
Understanding the animal kingdom

One day, while visiting a third-grade classroom, I displayed a full-color photo-poster of what might be the favorite, or at least the most attention getting, "pet" of recent years—the shark.

"Who can tell me what this is?" I asked through the "oohs" and "ahs."

Aron literally jumped out of his seat with anticipation, shouting, "It's Jaws!"

His answer couldn't be disputed. Peter Benchley, author of the best-selling novels, *Jaws* and *Jaws II,* had changed almost overnight the name of all sharks to Jaws!

Needless to say, the one book I had with me, *Hungry Sharks* by John F. Waters, with illustrations by Ann Dalton, was grabbed by Aron immediately. And a class reading/waiting list posted on the bulletin board was soon filled with 10 other "takers."

About a week later, a student panel discussed the multitude of facts they had learned about these water dwellers. Aron even knew the difference between a hammerhead and a Zambezi. The book had helped change their narrow concept of a shark as "jaws" to that of a complex and fascinating creature and supported my theory that nonfiction books are excellent reading motivators.

LEARN A CAMEL

You might begin a study of one specific creature by posting its picture on a bulletin board with a title such as "Facts About the _____." Encourage children to fill the board with information and drawings gleaned from their readings. This can be an ongoing project throughout the school year. You can change the animal monthly or whenever interest begins to lag. Each animal studied could be added to a "Class Wildlife Preserve" bulletin board or diorama.

The same idea can be used in middle and upper grades to integrate science with language arts. As students read, suggest they note facts about a particular animal on index cards; include such resource information as the title of the book, the author, illustrator, publisher, and publication date. Cards filed in an individual or class box will be invaluable for research projects. Valuable animal research can also be done "on location" at local zoos, wildlife preserves, or natural history museums.

A good source book that girls and boys will enjoy browsing through is *Animal Facts and Feats* by Gerald L. Wood, one of the "Guinness Family of Books." Literally thousands of amazing animal feats and achievements, including a chapter on "Extinct Animals," are cited, along with over 150 photographs, many in full color. An excellent index is appended.

Books about animal life can also be tied into the social studies curriculum. *The Hippopotamus Book* by Winifred Rosen Casey describes the hippo's important role in the chain of life in the rivers and deltas of Africa, thus introducing the concept of ecological balance. Visuals in full color by Greg and Tim Hildebrandt realistically depict the hippopotamus and its environment and include maps of the animals' African habitats.

Camels: Ships of the Desert, also by Waters, with illustrations by Reynold Ruffins, shows how the camel survives the harsh conditions of its habitat. The book could inspire a project on animals in other extreme environments such as polar bears and penguins. Both ... *Sharks* and *Camels* ... are part of Thomas Y. Crowell's "Let's-Read-and-Find-Out Science Book" series. Other volumes focus on bats, bees, shrimp, spiders, frogs, and fireflies. Also in this series bonanza are paperbound editions, sound-filmstrip sets, and several titles offered in Spanish.

CATCH A STARFISH

During spring and summer, insects emerge—crickets chatter, ants lug and load, bees buzz busily. It is the season to study wildlife and insect life. Discuss the idea that good "petmanship" means knowing about and understanding particular animals' needs.

Begin developing pet-care awareness by introducing *Pets in a Jar: Collecting and Caring for Small Wild Animals* by Seymour Simon. The narrative explains how children, with little experience, can find, catch, and keep many small animals as pets, including water bugs, starfish, brine shrimp, and pond snails. Illustrations are by Betty Fraser. After discussing some of these tiny creatures, ask children: "How would you like living in a mayonnaise jar when there is nature to explore?" Help students understand that they can learn a lot about pets in a jar, but after a short time they should let the pets go free.

Continue your minispecies study with ants, which are easy to come by in warm weather. *Questions and Answers About Ants* by Millicent E. Selsam is chock-full of information based on the author's observations of an ant colony. Where do you find ants? What do they eat? How do they sleep? How do you keep them? Questions such as these are expertly answered. Illustrations are by Arabelle Wheatley.

Younger insect observers and collectors will enjoy *I Like Beetles* by Gladys Conklin, which describes the distinguishing characteristics of 29 beetles from the swimming whirligig beetle to the African boliath, which is almost as big as a child's hand. Or suggest *Catch A Cricket* by Carla Stevens, an easy-to-read book that tells how to capture and care for crickets, grasshoppers, fireflies, worms, and caterpillars, illustrated with photographs.

Temporary classroom insect collections provide an opportunity for student entomologists to record changes in their insects' appearance, eating habits, and all aspects of their environment. Often a simple question such as: "What makes a beetle a beetle?" will help youngsters develop classifying and critical thinking skills.

ANIMAL COMMUNICATION

Foxes are sly, raccoons are mischievous, puppies are playful, donkeys are lazy, fish are dumb—or are they? How much do your students really know about animal behavior?

From the time human beings appeared on the earth, they have been fascinated with animal behavior—observing and drawing conclusions on animal life. But it wasn't until the early part of the twentieth century, via the work of Austrian psychologist Konrad Zacharius Lorenz, that the scientific study of animal behavior, ethology, evolved. With patience, sharp eyes and ears, and a number of fascinating books, children can conduct their own studies of animals, especially regarding the way they communicate.

Listen to the Animals

Categorizing the sounds of a pet cat, dog, or bird is one simple way of learning how it passes information to other animals or humans. Ask student volunteers to tape-record such sounds and make notes as to the time of day and the circumstances under which the sounds were uttered. When students play the recordings in class, it will be interesting to see if classmates can tell the difference, for example, between the sounds of two canaries or can identify the sound of a hungry cat.

A fascinating volume on one pet's form of communication is *What Is Your Dog Saying?* by Dr. Michael Fox and Wende Devlin Gates. An informative, lively, question-and-answer format explains how to interpret canine messages from puppyhood to old age. Illustrated with black-and-white photographs, the book includes charts on choosing a dog and a dog's body language.

The various meanings of purring, twitching tails, and other feline language is presented in *How to Talk to Your Cat* by Patricia Moyes, illustrated by Nancy Lou Gahan. Although this is an adult book, mature readers will enjoy the fascinating information presented.

Cheeps, Chirps, and Buzzes

Observing the wilder species adds a new dimension to a study of animal behavior and communication. But children won't have to trek to a forest if their subjects are wild birds, from city pigeons and sparrows to country wrens and cardinals. A quiet place outdoors where birds gather, patience, and a tape recorder are all they need. Again, have them take notes describing the birds and characteristic movements, time, place, and weather conditions. Back in class, students can research the species they observed, draw and cut out original illustrations, and attach the findings to a bulletin board display entitled "Bird Concerts." Drawings can be numbered to coincide with cassette tapes. To further probe the mysteries of bird songs, calls, and noises, refer to *Bird Talk* by Roma Gans, illustrated by Jo Polenso. Included are descriptions of calls of a few common northeastern woodland birds such as the blue jay, English sparrow, cardinal, and wood thrush. Also part of Crowell's "Let's-Read-and-Find-Out Science Book" series, this is written in an easy-to-read style.

Sounds of Animals at Night by Edward R. Ricciuti is another easy-to-read volume for middle to upper graders. The author gives a guide to the language of birds, as well as frogs, toads, insects, and mammals, that prefer nocturnal to diurnal life. Descriptions of mating calls, warning sounds, weather prediction behaviors, and the temperature indicator sounds of insects are just some of the intriguing aspects of this book.

Sea Creatures

Unless students live near an aquarium, which is always a favorite field trip adventure, it isn't likely that they will be able to study sea animals. But they can discover oceans of information from the following excellent titles dealing with these popular creatures. Students might want to split up into small groups, each choosing an animal and then sharing their research with the class via individual presentations or panel discussions.

Sounds in the Sea by Francine Jacobs provides an introduction to marine bioacoustics, the study of sounds and hearing abilities of marine animals. The author reports on the strange snapping, thumping, and crushing sounds of certain fish and crustacea, how and why they make these noises, and the methods used to detect them. The last chapter deals with the hearing capacities of certain marine mammals and how they can be useful to humans. Wonderful anecdotes are accompanied by black-and-white illustrations by Jean Zallinger. What child wouldn't be fascinated to know, for example, that sea horses snap loudly in response to various changes, female porpoises whistle to summon other females when they are about to give birth, or that humpback whales may "speak" in regional dialects? (Humpback whales from Puerto Rico, for instance, have different accents from those of the Bahama and Virgin Islands.) An index is included.

Playing recordings of actual sea mammal sounds will hold students spellbound. Two of these are *Song of the Humpback Whale* and *Deep Voices,* both distributed by Capitol Records. Use these recordings along with *Whales: Their Life in the Sea* by Faith McNulty. This volume describes various kinds of whales—how they communicate across great distances, care for their young, and annually make extraordinary journeys from the polar ice to warmer regions. The last chapter is a plea to save whales from extinction from their greatest enemy— humans. Dramatic black-and-white drawings are by John Schoenherr; a bibliography and index are appended.

No study of marine animals would be complete without the shark, well represented in the previously mentioned *Hungry Sharks* by Waters. The volume simply details the animal's fine sensory awareness—an acute sense of smell and the ability to see at night, hear the underwater sounds other fish make, and even feel movements in the water—which it uses to satisfy its unending appetite. Another easy-to-read source, done in question-and-answer format, is *Sharks* by Ann McGovern, illustrated by Murray Tinkelman.

DEDICATED ANIMAL WATCHERS

In a class by itself is *Wild Animals, Gentle Women* by Margery Facklam, illustrated with line drawings by Paul Facklam and black-and-white photographs. This book relates the experiences of 11 women who have dedicated their lives to animal-watching, including Jane Goodall, who advanced the study of chimpanzees by observing them in the Gombe Stream Reserve on the shores of Lake Tanganyika in Africa; Ruth Harkness, who ventured to China in 1936 to study the *bei-shung* (giant panda), an animal no one had ever seen alive outside of China; and Kay McKeever, who founded the Owl Research and Rehabilitation Center in Ontario, the only one of its kind in North America. This fine text, which could be useful to develop awareness of animal-related careers, offers vast amounts of information in highly readable prose. A three-page bibliography and a listing of eight "Organizations to Help You Learn About Animal Watching" is appended.

DOMESTIC PETS

Many children's best friends are domestic pets. To initiate a pets project, poll the class to find out how many and what types of pets they have. If possible, have the children bring in photographs of pets and plan a "Pets on Parade" bulletin-board display. You might also ask students to discuss the pleasures and problems involved in animal care and training.

Being a pet owner entails important responsibilities. Whether your students already have pets or are thinking of acquiring one, they can glean much information on how to keep a pet happy and healthy from the following nonfiction titles.

Dogs and Cats

The miracle of the birth and growth of puppies is beautifully depicted in *My Puppy Is Born* by Joanna Cole. The simple text and excellent black-and-white photographs by Jerome Wexler record the first eight weeks in the life of Sausage, a miniature dachsund. Younger readers will also enjoy looking at *Life Begins for Puppies* by Lilo Hess. The author relates the story of Poco, a dog she adopts from a local animal shelter and soon finds out is pregnant. The book tells of the birth and the first eight weeks of Poco's four puppies. Accurate and detailed descriptions of the puppies' birth and development are given, accompanied by the author's sensitive and consistently fine black-and-white photographs.

A Puppy for You, also written and photographed by Hess, covers selection, care, feeding, housetraining, and grooming, and includes directions for training puppies to obey basic commands. Good black-and-white photographs portray some of the many breeds of dogs. An index is included.

For older readers, a concise, easy-to-follow guide to puppy care is *Superpuppy: How to Choose, Raise and Train the Best Possible Dog for You,* written and illustrated by Jill and D. Manus Pinkwater. Enlivened by personal anecdotes and numerous illustrations, the volume takes a philosophical approach to the latest facts about owning and raising a dog. A booklist is appended, along with an index and a directory of organizations that can supply additional information. The Pinkwaters, who operate a dog school called "Superpuppy" in Hoboken, New Jersey, provide a nice touch by inviting readers to send in questions regarding training problems not covered in the book—another letter-writing opportunity!

Another title they will enjoy is *Bringing Up Puppies: A Child's Book of Dog Breeding and Care* by Jane Whitbread Levin, which is based on the experience of four children who bred a black cocker spaniel and watched her whelp four puppies. This practical guide answers many of the questions connected with breeding. Black-and-white photographs are by Mary Morris Steiner. An index is included.

Young cat lovers will enjoy *How Kittens Grow* by Millicent E. Selsam, in which charming black-and-white photographs by Esther Bubley show the growth stages of four newborn kittens. The book is also available in a Spanish edition under the title *Cómo Crecen los Gatitos,* translated by Argentina Palacios.

For older readers, there is *Catnip: Selecting and Training Your Cat* by Kurt Unkelbach, illustrated by Haris Petie. After presenting a brief history of cats, the author discusses the pure breeds recognized in the United States. A rather short but interesting chapter relates "Myths About Cats." A glossary, anatomy charts, and listings of cat associations and magazines are appended.

Fish

Fish are not known for returning their owners' affection and admiration, but their small environments and silent, tranquil movements make them ideal household members. An excellent guide for beginners on how to keep aquarium waters untroubled for tropical fish is *A Great Aquarium Book* by Jane Sarnoff, illustrated by Reynold Ruffins. Although the thrust of the book is ecological, emphasizing that fish are living creatures, not toys and decorations, the author has meshed the factual information with nonsensical fun throughout the text and illustrations. Four fishes for this one!

Two other fishy titles to consult are *What Do You Want to Know About Guppies?* by Seymour Simon, illustrated by Susan Bonners, and *All About Goldfish as Pets* by Kay Cooper, illustrated with black-and-white photographs by Alvin E. Staffan.

Horses

Just reading about horses can be almost as delightful as the thought of owning one. Four well-bred books on their care, feeding, and lifestyles will hold valuable places in any equine library.

Birth of a Foal by Jane Miller is an explicit photo-story of the birth of Fizz, a Welsh Mountain pony, and her first few days of life. In *A Pony to Love,* Lilo Hess describes several types of ponies, how to select one, and what is needed for proper care. The text is illustrated with the author's black-and-white photographs. Both of these attractive books will appeal to young readers.

Horse Happy: A Complete Guide to Owning Your First Horse by Barbara J. Berry, with black-and-white photographs by James Dandelski and black-and-white line drawings by Terry Nell Morris, is a well-written, inviting volume for the many children who are afflicted with the wonderfully incurable condition of being "horse happy"—wanting a horse more than anything else in the world. As the author points out, almost half of the fun is in the long-term planning of horse ownership; sound advice is offered for children to reach that goal. Topics dealt with include choosing the right horse, "dealing" with horse dealers, building or remodeling a barn (or finding a suitable boarding stable), buying and maintaining good tack and equipment, finding and keeping a good veterinarian and farrier, and establishing daily routines for chores needed to be done. Various breeds and basic pointers on riding and training are also discussed. An excellent seven-page glossary, a two-page bibliography, and five-page index are appended.

A Very Young Rider, written and photographed by Jill Krementz, is a splendid volume. The easy-to-read text and 169 dramatic black-and white photographs show 10-year-old Vivi Malloy's strong relationship with her pony, Ready Penny, and her dedication and sense of responsibility as she strives toward professional riding competition.

OTHER PERFECT PETS

Comprehensive information on keeping and caring for a wide variety of pets is presented to amateur zoologists in the following: *Amphibians as Pets* by Georg and Lisbeth Zappler; *Birds as Pets* by Paul Villiard; *All About Rabbits as Pets* by Kay Cooper; *Hamsters: All About Them; Guinea Pigs: All About Them* and *Rabbits: All About Them* by Dr. Alvin and Virginia B. Silverstein; and *Keeping Insects as Pets* by Ross and Pat Olney.

Two volumes that also offer a great deal of information are *Perfect Pets* by Francene and Louis Sabin, and the large-sized paperback, *Great Pets: An Extraordinary Guide to Usual and Unusual Family Pets* by Sara Stein.

SPECIAL PET BOOKS

When children have completed their search for pet information, they might design their own "Pet Book" along the lines of popular baby books. Individual sections can show various stages of development with photographs or original drawings and others can feature hand-made birth certificates, paw prints, swatches of hair or fur, medical information, and family background. These take-home projects will be treasured long after the child and pet are fully grown.

REFERENCES[1]

Berry, Barbara J. *Horse Happy: A Complete Guide to Owning Your First Horse.* Bobbs-Merrill, 1978.

Casey, Winifred J. *The Hippopotamus Book.* Western, 1975.

Cole, Joanna. *My Puppy Is Born.* Morrow, 1973.

Conklin, Gladys. *I Like Beetles.* Holiday House, 1975.

Cooper, Kay. *All About Goldfish As Pets.* Messner, 1976.

———. *All About Rabbits As Pets.* Messner, 1974.

Facklam, Margery. *Wild Animals, Gentle Women.* Harcourt, 1978.

Fox, Dr. Michael, and Wendy Devlin Gates. *What Is Your Dog Saying?* Coward, McCann, 1977.

Gans, Roma. *Bird Talk.* Crowell, 1971.

Hess, Lilo. *A Pony to Love.* Scribner, 1975.

———. *A Puppy for You.* Scribner, 1975; also available in paperback.

———. *Life Begins for Puppies.* Scribner, 1975.

Jacobs, Francine. *Sounds in the Sea.* Morrow, 1977.

Krementz, Jill. *A Very Young Rider.* Knopf, 1977.

Levin, Jane Whitbread. *Bringing Up Puppies: A Child's Book of Dog Breeds and Care.* Harcourt, 1958.

McGovern, Ann. *Sharks.* Four Winds, 1976; Scholastic paperback.

McNulty, Faith. *Whales: Their Life in the Sea.* Harper & Row, 1975.

Miller, Jane. *Birth of a Foal.* Lippincott, 1977.

Moyes, Patricia. *How to Talk to Your Cat.* Holt, Rinehart and Winston, 1978.

[1]See Appendix for publishers' complete addresses.

Olney, Ross, and Pat Olney. *Keeping Insects as Pets.* Watts, 1978.

Palacios, Argentina, trans. *Cómo Crecen los Gatitos.* Scholastic paperback.

Pinkwater, Jill, and D. Manus Pinkwater. *Superpuppy: How to Choose, Raise and Train the Best Possible Dog for You.* Seabury, 1977.

Ricciuti, Edward R. *Sounds of Animals at Night.* Harper & Row, 1977.

Sabin, Francene, and Louis Sabin. *Perfect Pets.* Putnam, 1978.

Sarnoff, Jane. *A Great Aquarium Book.* Scribner, 1977; also available in paperback.

Selsam, Millicent E. *How Kittens Grow.* Four Winds, 1975; Scholastic paperback.

———. *Questions and Answers About Ants.* Four Winds, 1967; Scholastic paperback.

Silverstein, Dr. Alvin, and Virginia B. Silverstein. *Guinea Pigs: All About Them.* Lothrop, 1972.

———. *Hamsters: All About Them.* Lothrop, 1974.

———. *Rabbits: All About Them.* Lothrop, 1973.

Simon, Seymour. *Pets in a Jar: Collecting and Caring for Small Wild Animals.* Viking, 1975.

———. *What Do You Want to Know About Guppies?* Four Winds, 1977.

Stein, Sara. *Great Pets: An Extraordinary Guide to Usual and Unusual Family Pets.* Workman, 1976; available in paperback.

Stevens, Carla. *Catch a Cricket.* Young Scott, 1961.

Unkelbach, Kurt. *Catnip: Selecting and Training Your Cat.* Prentice-Hall, 1970; also available in paperback.

Villiard, Paul. *Birds as Pets.* Doubleday, 1974.

Waters, John F. *Camels: Ships of the Desert.* Crowell, 1974.

———. *Hungry Sharks.* Crowell, 1973.

Wood, Gerald L. *Animal Facts and Feats.* Sterling, 1977; Bantam paperback.

Zappler, Georg, and Lisbeth Zappler. *Amphibians as Pets.* Doubleday, 1973.

PART VIII

Last, but Certainly not Least

31

Counting to 100 — and well beyond

At a recent visit to my sister's house, my 5-year-old niece, Jennifer, greeted me and beamed with some newfound knowledge.

"Know what?" she asked.

"What?" I asked back.

"I can count to 100—one, two, three, four, five, six, seven, eight...."

I hadn't the heart to stop her, so she continued—through the other greetings, the hanging up of coats, and on and on until she finally reached the magic, "100!"

I applauded. It was a mistake.

"Want to hear it again?" she asked.

"No!" I immediately exclaimed. "Once is enough!"

Jennifer, in her own youthful way, had discovered numbers —a giant step for every human being. But math lessons needn't always be as rote as counting from one to 100. The world of children's books offers many opportunities to go beyond necessary basic, but routine lessons and gives children the incentive to explore math in different and practical ways.

MIXING MATH WITH FREE VERSE

One of my favorite ways to launch math lessons—whether I am introducing basic addition facts or teaching girls and boys the importance of fractions—is with Carl Sandburg's wonderful nine-stanza poem, "Arithmetic." The quite popular poem, telling of the ups and downs of math, can be found in two outstanding anthologies, *Reflections on a Gift of Watermelon Pickle and Other Modern Verse,* compiled by Stephen Dunning, Edward Lueders, and Hugh Smith; and *The Sandburg Treasury: Prose and Poetry for Young People* by Carl Sandburg, with illustrations by Paul Bacon. This is one poem that you will want to use over and over again with students of all ages and grade levels.

MOTHER GOOSE COMPUTATIONS

A trip to almost any library will yield a countless number of "Mother Goose" collections, many illustrated by master artists. Several popular collections of Mother Goose rhymes include *Gregory Griggs and Other Nursery Rhyme People,* selected and illustrated by Arnold Lobel; *The Mother Goose Book,* selected and illustrated by Alice and Martin Provenson; *Granfa' Grif Had a Pig and other Rhymes Without Reason from Mother Goose*, compiled and illustrated by Wallace Tripp; and *Brian Wildsmith's Mother Goose: A Collection of Nursery Rhymes.*

As children read and reread Mother Goose favorites, have them note the rhymes containing numbers and encourage them to make up individual word problems for classmates to solve. For example, "How many men went to sea in a bowl?" (Three.) "Add this number to the number of bags of wool the black sheep had." (Three.) "What is the answer?" (Six.)

With numberless rhymes, children can have great fun studying various illustrators' interpretations. For example, how many silver bells and cockle shells can they find pictured in Contrary Mary's garden? How many children lived in the old woman's shoe? Not only will girls and boys be reading these treasured literary classics, they will be doing simple math problems and perusing artwork by some of the top illustrators of children's books in the country.

THAT'S ENTERTAINMENT! THAT'S MATH

A wide variety of entertaining books that teach various math principles can provide countless hours of enjoyment and practice for students. For example, with younger readers try *Funny Number Tricks: Easy Magic with Arithmetic* by Rose Wyler and Gerald Ames. The tricks are easy-to-learn using readily available materials, such as paper, cards, coins, and dominoes, and involve simple addition and subtraction facts. The volume, divided into three parts and engagingly illustrated by Talavaldis Stubis, can be used to spark classroom magical mathematics shows for peers or parents.

Another volume for younger readers that can be used to motivate "math thinking" is *How to Count Sheep Without Falling to Sleep*. Written by Ralph Leighton, a math teacher, and his young teenaged student, Carl Feynman, it presents a fabricated history of numbers that is designed to show how various properties of our number system were discovered and applied. The authors' concept of using symbols for numbers is a delightful model for girls and boys who want to devise their own original numeration systems. The text is illustrated by George Ulrich.

The I Hate Mathematics! Book by Marilyn Burns, illustrated by Martha Hairston, reflects a popular feeling among many. But the math events, gags, riddles, experiments, and tricks offered in this book can change almost anyone from a math denouncer to a devotee. Chapters include "How to Always Be a Winner," "Things to Do When You Have the Flu," and "Street Math."

An excellent addition to middle- and upper-grade math libraries is *The Ages of Mathematics*, a four-volume series edited by Charles F. Linn. Subtitles include: Volume I, *The Origins* by Michael Moffat; Volume II, *Mathematics East and West* by Linn; Volume III, *Western Mathematics Comes of Age* by Cynthia Crowell Cook; and Volume IV, *The Modern Ages* by Peter D. Cook. The books present a nontechnical survey dealing with the history of math from its simplest beginnings through to its modern complexities, covering a broad scope of topics from counting systems in primary societies to the computer revolution. Numerous personalities and their contributions to the world of math (such as Lewis Carroll and Albert Einstein) are also woven into the lively, conversational texts; each volume contains an index. The series can well be used for social studies tie-ins.

METRIC POWER

With metric usage becoming more commonplace, you'll have no trouble finding a variety of titles to explain the system's workings. A different approach, however, is offered via *Metric Can Be Fun!*, written and illustrated by Munro Leaf. This book provides a simple introduction to the practical use of the metric system, while involving young readers in measuring length in meters, liquids in liters, and weight in grams. It also describes temperature measurement with the Celsius thermometer and includes conversion charts. The simplicity of the text and the black-and-white line drawings will appeal to reluctant readers, as well as reluctant mathemeticians. For older readers, *Metric: The Modern Way to Measure* by Miriam Schlein traces the development of measuring systems, poses an argument in favor of the United States' conversion, and provides conversion charts. The volume is illustrated in cartoon-like drawings by Jan Pyk.

The "Metrics America" series by Jerolyn Ann Nentl includes five titles providing readers with a true ground-floor understanding of the system. Titles are well designed with descriptive black-and-white and full-color illustrations. Readers are encouraged to measure their beds, lawns, and other familiar items, construct a liter box, and make a balance scale.

A unique offering also for middle and upper graders is *Metric Puzzles* by Peggy and Irving Adler. Students who enjoy crossword puzzles, anagrams, and word exercises will be challenged and informed by 52 games based on basic metric vocabulary and symbols. Clear, easy-to-read conversion tables are appended.

For the mature reader, steer toward *The Metric System* by Joan Elma Rahn, which emphasizes learning the system by using it, giving units meaning, rather than just converting them from the customary system. This highly readable, well-designed volume with black-and-white line drawings by Ginny Linville Winter contains an extensive appendix containing conversion tables.

MATH IN OTHER MEDIA

In addition to books galore, there are other types of media that enhance math study, particularly for individualized learning and/or learning centers. Two file boxes geared to upper graders include *Projects for the Math Lab* by Shirley S. Price and *Projects in Metric Measurement* by Shirley and Merle E. Price. Each box contains over 100 activity cards with student directions on how to tackle problems using easy-to-obtain materials.

Dozens of inviting titles make up the "Crowell Young Math Books" series. Readers of all ages can explore such diverse areas as geometry and topology, algebra, logic, and applied math. Many of the titles are also available in paperback editions; several have accompanying sound–color filmstrip sets. For a complete listing of titles, send a self-addressed, stamped large manila envelope requesting the free "Crowell Young Math Books" brochure.

You can expect a stampede to the math center if you offer the four-part sound filmstrip series *Donald in Mathemagic Land* produced by Walt Disney Educational Media Company. The hyperactive duck in this award-winning set, based on the popular 16 mm. character of the same name, presents a dazzling approach to math for intermediate-grade and even high school students. The filmstrips explore the importance of math in music, art, and ideas. Students travel with Donald Duck through "Mathemagic Land" where trees have square roots, and Pythagoras has a musical "jam" session. The journey introduces students to many basic mathematical concepts. The golden rectangle, golden spiral, musical scale, and the secrets of the pentagram are a few of the subjects analyzed. The filmstrips, comprehensive teacher's guide, and record or cassette soundtrack provide valuable lessons in an entertaining format.

Liking and learning math don't have to be at the opposite ends of the spectrum. Books and other media that reveal the subject's many fascinating aspects can compatibly unite interest and skills.

REFERENCES[1]

Adler, Peggy, and Irving Adler. *Metric Puzzles.* Watts, 1977.

Donald in Mathemagic Land (filmstrip set). Walt Disney Educational Media Company.

Dunning, Stephen, Edward Lueders, and Hugh Smith. *Reflections on a Gift of Watermelon Pickle and Other Modern Verse.* Scott, Foresman, 1966.

Leaf, Munro. *Metric Can Be Fun!* Lippincott, 1976.

Leighton, Ralph, and Carl Feynman. *How to Count Sheep Without Falling Asleep.* Prentice-Hall, 1976.

[1]See Appendix for publishers' complete addresses.

Linn, Charles E., ed. *The Ages of Mathematics* series. Doubleday, 1977.
  Cook, Cynthia Crowell. *Western Mathematics Comes of Age,* Vol.
  III.
  Cook, Peter D. *The Modern Ages,* Vol. IV.
  Linn, Charles E. *Mathematics East and West,* Vol. II.
  Moffatt, Michael. *The Origins,* Vol. I.
Lobel, Arnold. *Gregory Griggs and Other Nursery Rhyme People.*
  Greenwillow, 1978.
Nentl, Jerolyn Ann. *Metrics America* series. Crestwood House, 1976.
  The Metric System Is.
  The Meter Is.
  The Liter is.
  The Gram Is.
  The Celsius Thermometer Is.
Price, Shirley S. *Projects for the Math Lab* (kit). Creative Teaching
  Press.
———, and Merle E. Price. *Projects in Metric Measurement* (kit). Cre-
  ative Teaching Press.
Provenson, Alice, and Martin Provenson. *The Mother Goose Book.*
  Random House, 1976.
Rahn, Joan Elma. *The Metric System.* Atheneum, 1975.
Sandburg, Carl. *The Sandburg Treasury: Prose and Poetry for Young
  People.* Harcourt, 1970.
Schlein, Miriam. *Metric: The Modern Way to Measure.* Harcourt, 1975;
  also available in paperback.
Tripp, Wallace. *Granfa' Grig Had A Pig and Other Rhymes without
  Reason from Mother Goose.* Little, Brown, 1976; also available in
  paperback.
Wildsmith, Brian. *Mother Goose: A Collection of Nursery Rhymes.*
  Watts, 1964.
Wyler, Rose, and Gerald Ames. *Funny Number Tricks: Easy Magic
  with Arithmetic.* Parents' Magazine, 1976.

Appendix:
Publisher's Complete Addresses

ABINGDON PRESS, 201 Eighth Ave. S., Nashville, TN 37202

ADDISON-WESLEY PUBLISHING CO., INC., Jacob Way, Reading, MA 01867

ARCHWAY, 1220 Ave. of the Americas, NY, NY 10020

ATHENEUM PUBLISHERS, 122 E. 42nd St., NY, NY 10017

AVON BOOKS, 959 Eighth Ave., NY, NY 10019

BANTAM BOOKS, INC., 666 Fifth Ave., NY, NY 10019

BOBBS-MERRILL CO., INC., 4300 W. 62nd St., Indianapolis, IN 46206

BONIM BOOKS, 80 Fifth Ave., NY, NY 10011

CENTER FOR APPLIED RESEARCH IN EDUCATION, INC., P.O. Box 130, W. Nyack, NY 10994

CHILDREN'S PRESS, 1224 W. Van Buren St., Chicago, IL 60607

COLLINS+WORLD: William Publishing Co., Inc., 2080 W. 117th St., Cleveland, OH 44111

COWARD: Coward, McCann & Geoghegan, Inc., 200 Madison Ave., NY, NY 10016

CREATIVE TEACHING PRESS, 1900 Tyler St., Suite 22, S. El Monte, CA 91733

CRESTWOOD HOUSE, INC., P.O. Box 3427, Highway 66 S., Mankato, MN 56001

CROWELL: Thomas Y. Crowell Co. (see Harper & Row)

CROWN PUBLISHERS, INC., 1 Park Ave., NY, NY 10016

JOHN DAY (see T. Y. Crowell)

DELACORTE PRESS, 1 Dag Hammarskjold Plaza, NY, NY 10017

DELL PUBLISHING CO., INC. (see Delacorte)

DIAL: The Dial Press (see Delacorte)

DISNEY: Walt Disney Educational Media Co., 500 S. Buena Vista St.,
    Burbank, CA 91521
DODD, MEAD & CO., 79 Madison Ave., NY, NY 10016
DOUBLEDAY & CO., 277 Park Ave., NY, NY 10017
DUTTON: E. P. Dutton & Co., Inc., 2 Park Ave., NY, NY 10016
M. EVANS & CO., INC., 216 E. 49th St., NY, NY 10017
FARRAR: Farrar, Straus & Giroux, Inc., 19 Union Square W., NY, NY
    10017
FOLLETT PUBLISHING CO., 1010 W. Washington Blvd., Chicago, IL
    60607
FOUR WINDS PRESS, 50 W. 44th St., NY, NY 10036
GALE RESEARCH CO., Book Tower, Detroit, MI 48226
GARRARD PUBLISHING CO., 1607 N. Market St., Champaign, IL
    61820
GIANT PHOTOS, INC., Box 406, Rockford, IL 61105
GRAY PANTHERS, 3700 Chestnut St., Philadelphia, PA 19104
GREENWILLOW BOOKS, 105 Madison Ave., NY, NY 10016
GROSSETT & DUNLAP, INC., 51 Madison Ave., NY, NY 10010
HARCOURT: Harcourt Brace Jovanovich, Inc., 757 Third Ave., NY,
    NY 10017
HARPER & ROW, PUBLISHERS, INC., 10 E. 53rd St., NY, NY 10022
HARVEY HOUSE, INC., PUBLISHERS, 20 Waterside Plaza, NY, NY
    10010
HILL & WANG, INC. (see Farrar)
HOLIDAY HOUSE, INC., 18 E. 53rd St., NY, NY 10022
HOLT, RINEHART AND WINSTON, 383 Madison Ave., NY, NY 10017
HOUGHTON MIFFLIN CO., 1 Beacon St., Boston, MA 02107
KNOPF: Alfred A. Knopf, Inc. (see Random House)
LERNER PUBLICATIONS CO., 241 First Ave. N., Minneapolis, MN
    55401
LIPPINCOTT: J. B. Lippincott Co. (see Harper & Row)
LITTLE, BROWN & CO., 34 Beacon St., Boston, MA 02106
LIVERIGHT, 386 Park Ave. S., NY, NY 10016
LOTHROP: Lothrop, Lee & Shepard Co. (see Greenwillow)
MACMILLAN PUBLISHING CO., INC., 866 Third Ave., NY, NY 10022
MCGRAW-HILL BOOK CO., 1221 Ave. of the Americas, NY, NY 10020
MCKAY: David McKay Co., Inc., 750 Third Ave., NY, NY 10017
MESSNER: Julian Messner (see Simon & Schuster)
MILLER-BRODY PRODUCTIONS, INC. (see Random House)
MORROW: William Morrow & Co., Inc. (see Greenwillow)
NELSON: Elsevier/Nelson Books (see Dutton)
OXFORD UNIVERSITY PRESS, INC., 200 Madison Ave., NY, NY
    10016
PANTHEON BOOKS (see Random House)
PARENTS' MAGAZINE PRESS, 52 Vanderbilt Ave., NY, NY 10017
PARNASSUS PRESS, 4080 Halleck St., Emeryville, CA 94608

PHILLIPS: S. G. Phillips, Inc., 305 W. 86th St., NY, NY 10024
PHOENIX FILMS, INC., 470 Park Ave., S., NY, NY 10016
PLAYS, INC., 8 Arlington St., Boston, MA 02116
PRENTICE-HALL, INC., Englewood Cliffs, NJ 07632
PUTNAM: G. P. Putnam's Sons (see Coward)
RANDOM HOUSE, INC., 201 E. 50th St., NY, NY 10022
RUNNING PRESS, INC., 38 S. 19th St., Philadelphia, PA 19103
SCARECROW PRESS, 52 Liberty St., Metuchen, NJ 08840
SCHOCKEN BOOKS, INC. (see Coward)
SCHOLASTIC; SCHOLASTIC/CITATION (see Four Winds)
SCOTT, FORESMAN & CO., 1900 E. Lake Ave., Glenview, IL 60025
SCRIBNER: Charles Scribner's Sons, 597 Fifth Ave., NY, NY 10017
SEABURY: The Seabury Press, Inc. (see Houghton Mifflin)
SIMON & SCHUSTER, INC., 1230 Ave. of the Americas, NY, NY 10020
STERLING PUBLISHING CO., INC., 2 Park Ave., NY, NY 10016
VIKING PENGUIN, INC., 625 Madison Ave., NY, NY 10022
WALKER & CO., 720 Fifth Ave., NY, NY 10019
WARNE: Frederick Warne & Co., Inc., 101 Fifth Ave., NY, NY 10003
WATTS: Franklin Watts, Inc., 730 Fifth Ave., NY, NY 10019
WESTERN PUBLISHING CO., 1220 Mound Ave., Racine, WI 53404
WESTON WOODS STUDIOS, INC., Weston, CT 06880
THE WESTMINSTER PRESS, 905 Witherspoon Bldg., Philadelphia,
    PA 19107
WHITMAN: Albert Whitman & Co., 560 W. Lake St., Chicago, IL 60606
YOUNG SCOTT BOOKS (see Addison-Wesley)

Author, Illustrator, Name, and Title Index